# Table of Contents

D1605357

# Trace these lines with a crayon.
# Start at the puppy.

Left-to-right tracking; tracing

# Cut these lines.
# Start at the scissors.

stop          stop          stop

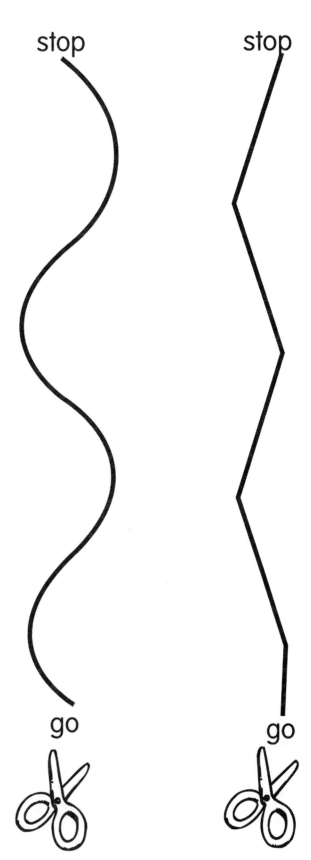

go          go          go

# Trace the balls.
# Color them.

Tracing and coloring; following directions

# Trace the fish.
# Color them.

Tracing and coloring; following directions

# Cut out the bears.
# Paste them in the wagon.

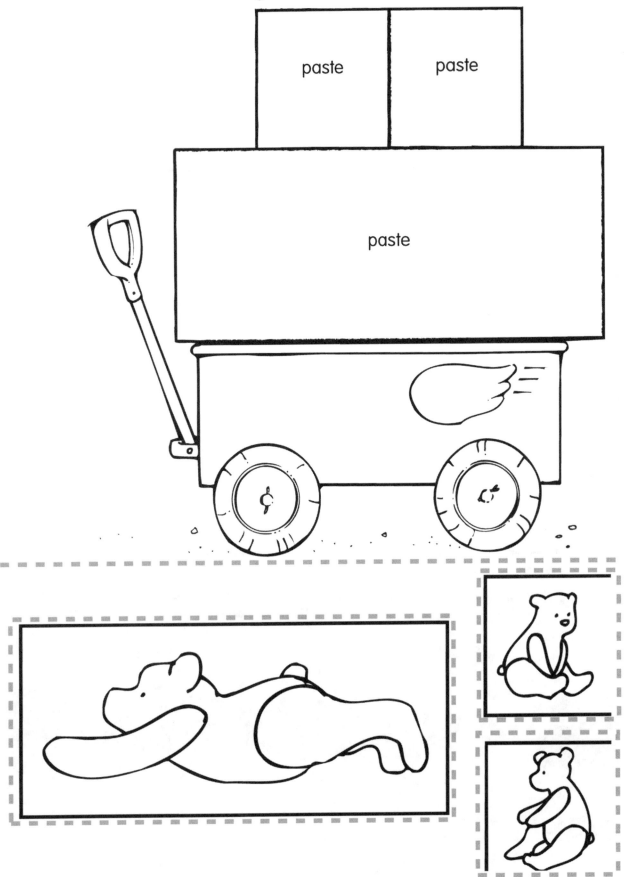

Using scissors; following directions

# Draw the wagon.
# Color it red.

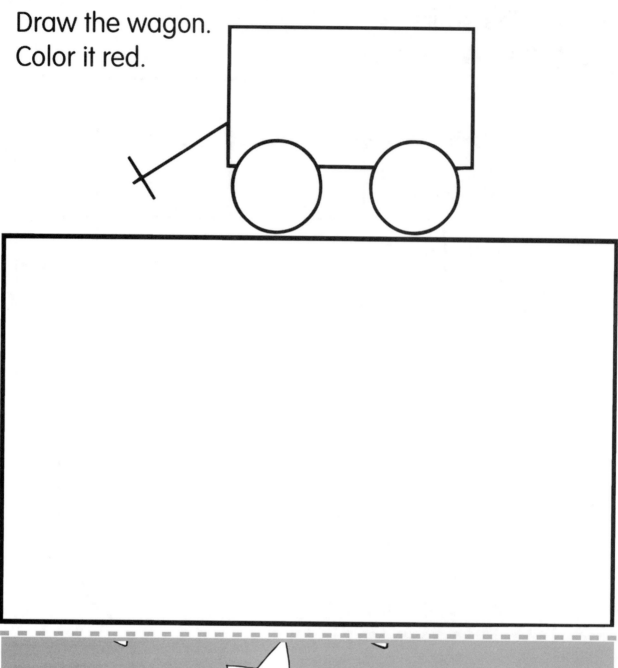

Drawing shapes; following directions

# Cut and paste.

Using scissors; following directions

Copy the ice cream cone.
Color it.

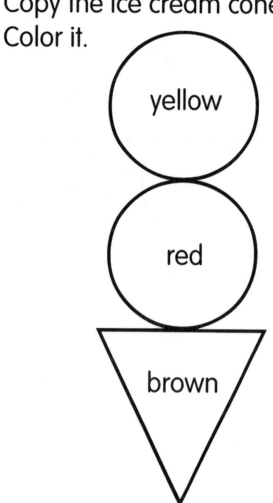

yellow

red

brown

Copying shapes

# Color the toys that are the same.

Classifying objects and pictures

# Match the birds that are the same.

Matching like objects and pictures

# Match the animals that are the same.

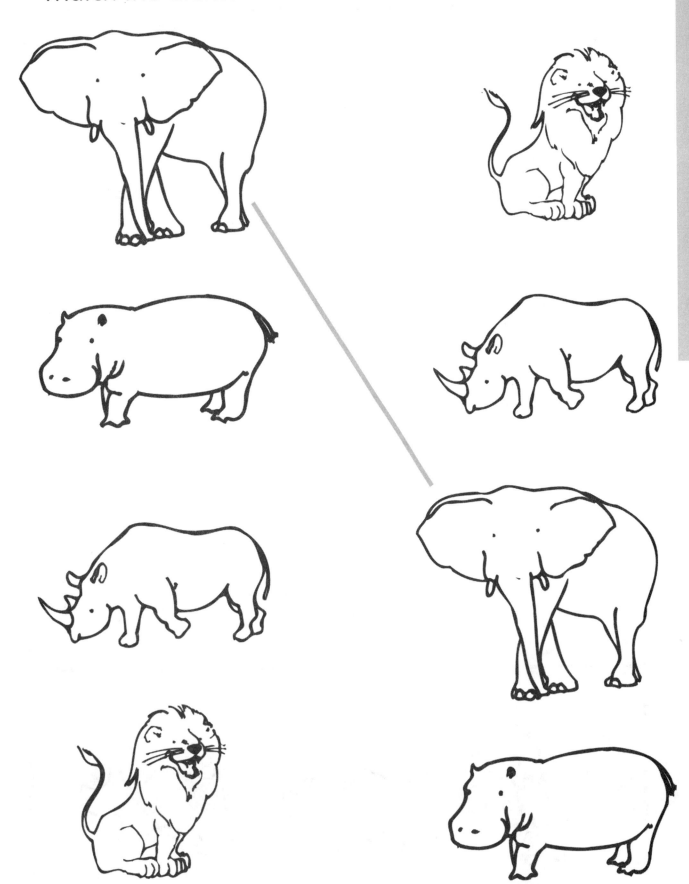

Matching like objects and pictures

# Color the pet that is different.

Classifying objects and pictures

# Make an X on the fruit that is different.

Classifying objects and pictures

# Color the things that go together.

Classifying objects and pictures

# Cut out the pictures.
# Put them in the correct boxes.

Classifying objects and pictures

# Color the bear.

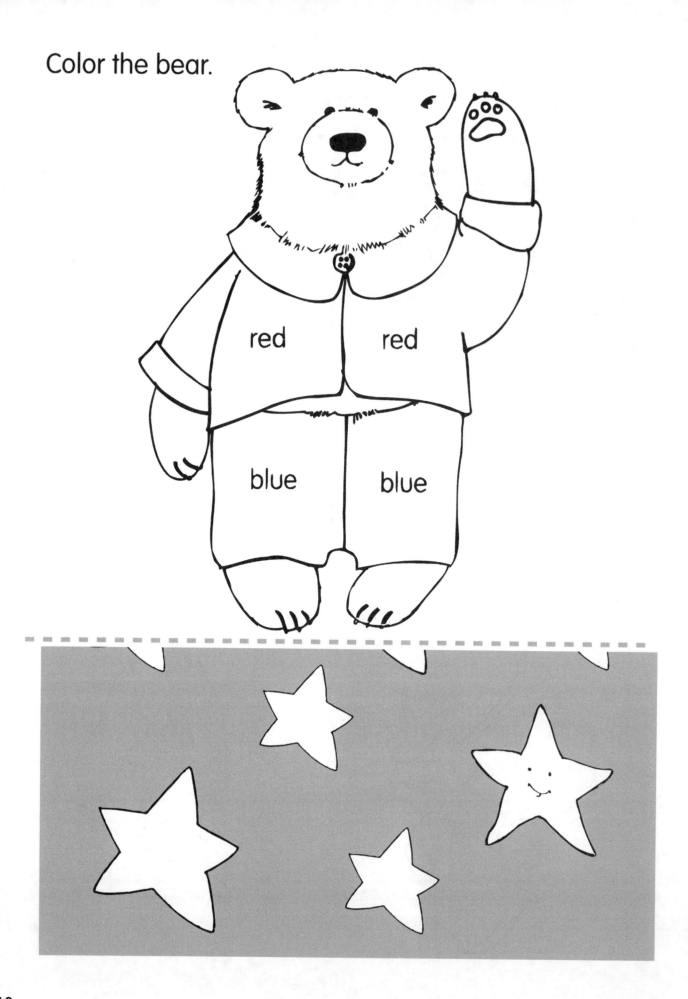

red red

blue blue

18    Recognizing color words

# Cut out the pictures.
# Paste them in the correct boxes.

# Trace and color the umbrella.

red

yellow

yellow

blue

Recognizing color words; tracing

# Color the things that go together.

Classifying objects and pictures

# Trace and write the letters.

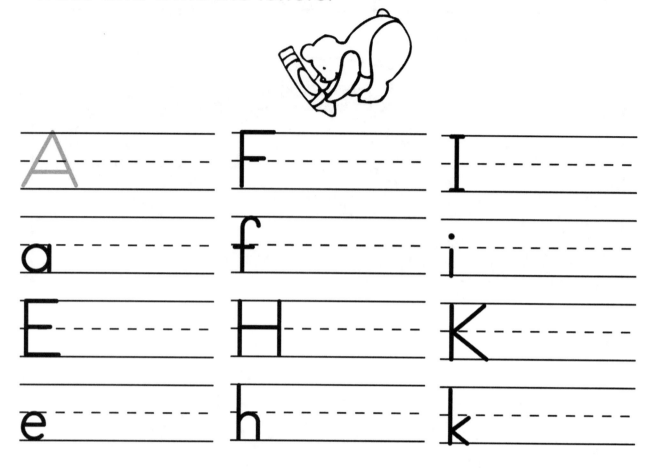

## Match the letters.

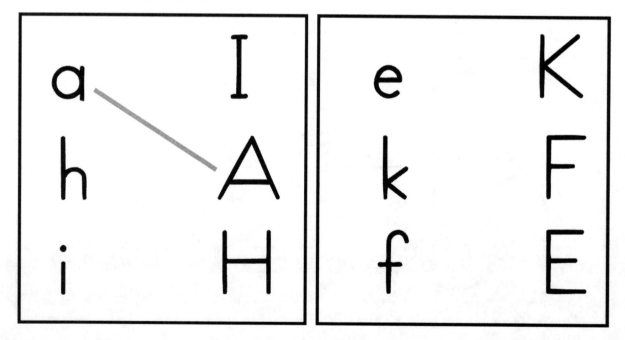

Tracing and writing letters; matching capital and lowercase letters

# Trace and write the letters.

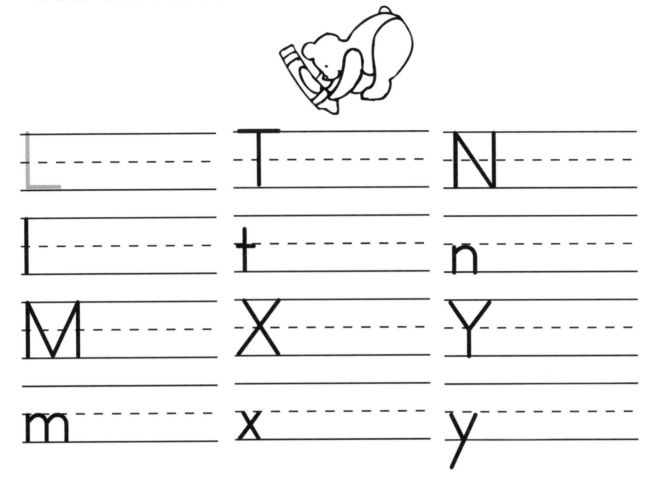

## Match the letters.

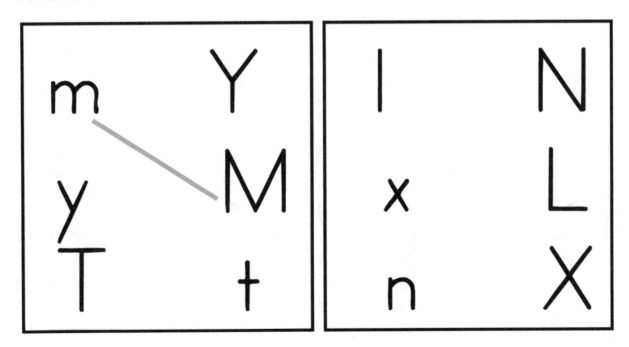

# Trace and write the letters.

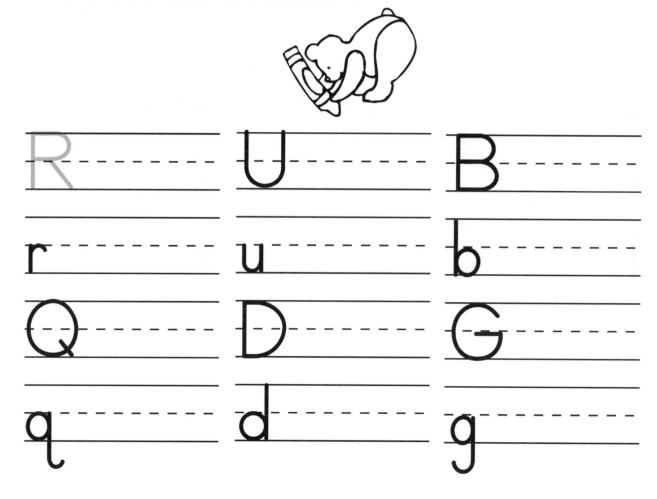

## Match the letters.

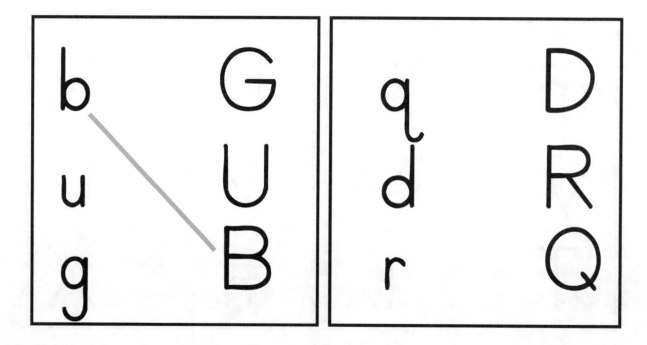

Tracing and writing letters; matching capital and lowercase letters

# Trace and write the letters.

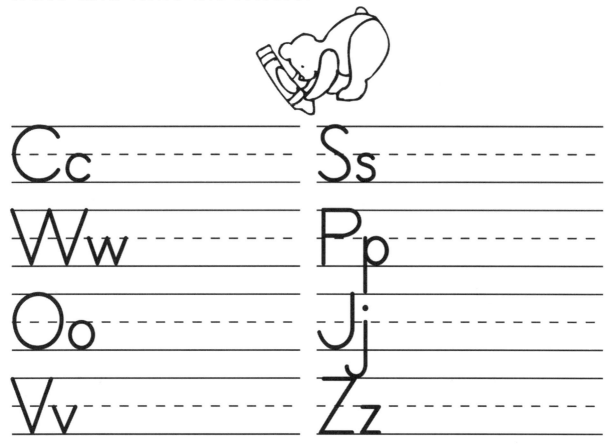

## Match the letters.

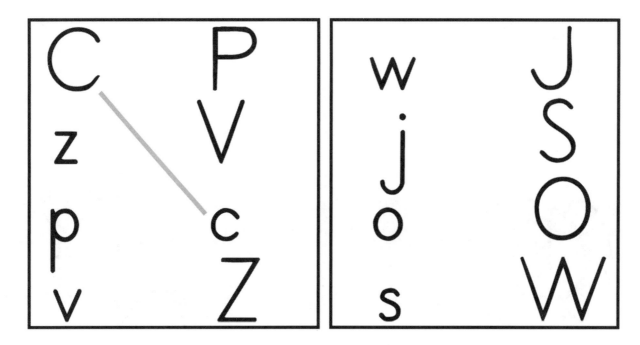

Tracing and writing letters; matching capital and lowercase letters

# Match the capital and lower case letters.

Matching capital and lowercase letters

# Cut out the letters.
# Paste them on the correct hat.

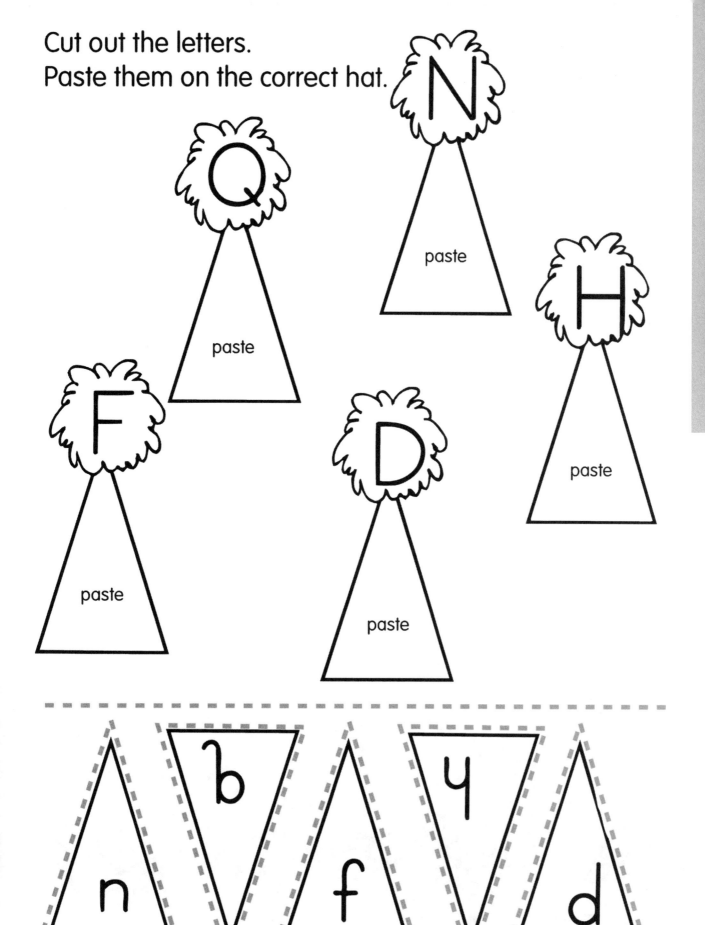

Copy the words.

pup

cow

ant

bell

Copying lowercase letters in words

Note: Write your child's first and last name so that it can be traced. Use a capital for the first letter and lower case letters for the rest of the name.

# Trace and write your first name.

# Trace and write your last name.

# Draw a picture of yourself.

# Connect the dots.
# Color the picture.

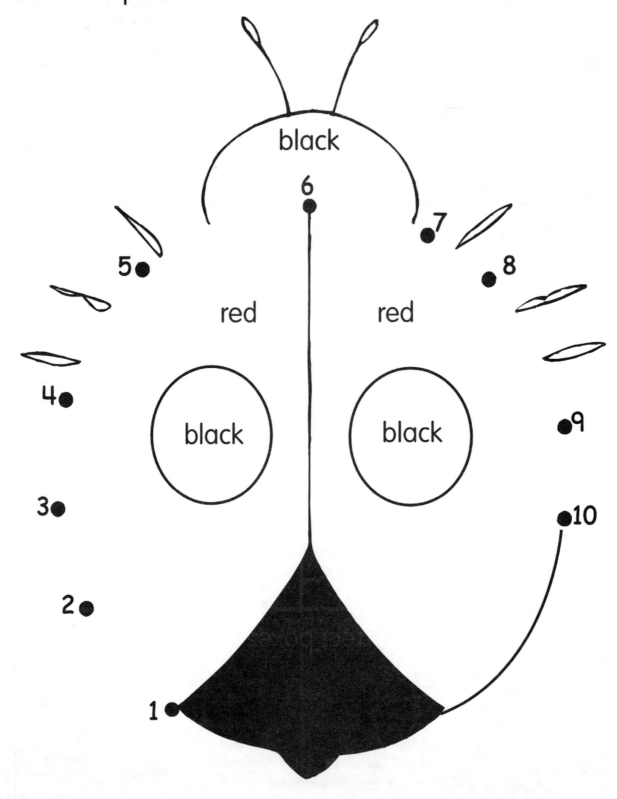

Understanding number order; recognizing color words

# Color and cut out the pictures.
## Paste them in order.

| 1 | 2 | 3 |
|---|---|---|
| paste | paste | paste |

# Color the kitten.

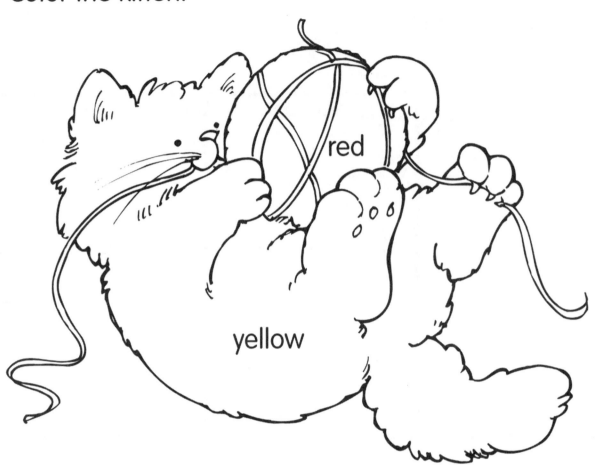

Recognizing color words

# Color and cut out the pictures.
# Paste them in order.

| 1 | 2 | 3 |
|---|---|---|
| paste | paste | paste |

# Connect the dots.
# Color the egg.

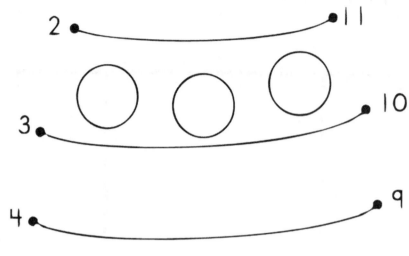

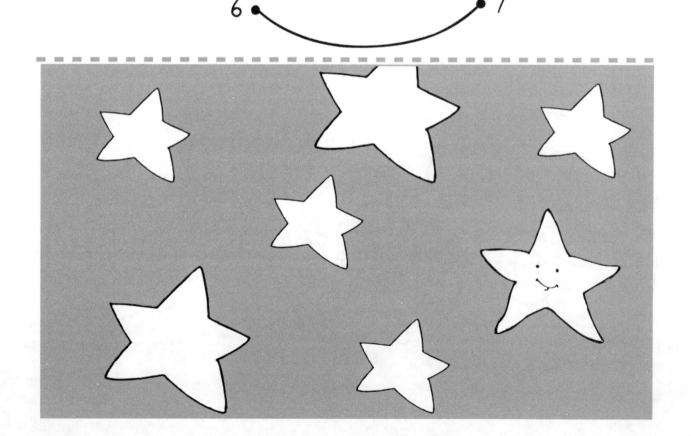

Understanding number order

# Color and cut out the pictures.
# Paste them in order.

| 1 | 2 | 3 |
|---|---|---|
| paste | paste | paste |

# Connect the dots.
# Draw a dog in the tub.

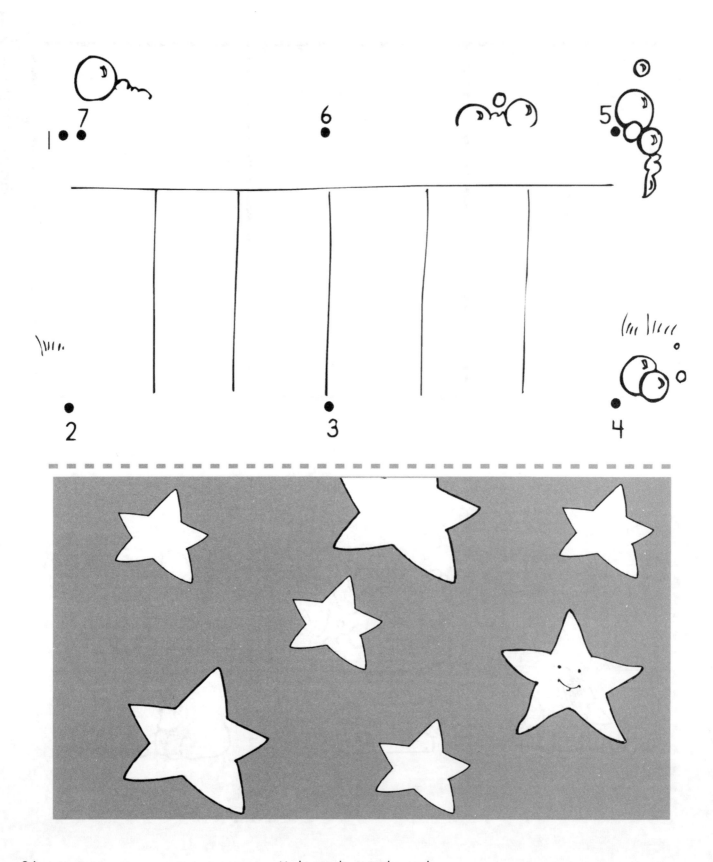

Understanding number order

# Color and cut out the pictures. Paste them in order.

| | |
|---|---|
| 1 <br><br><br> paste | 2 <br><br><br> paste |
| 3 <br><br><br> paste | 4 <br><br><br> paste |

# Draw a snowman. Use 3 ◯.

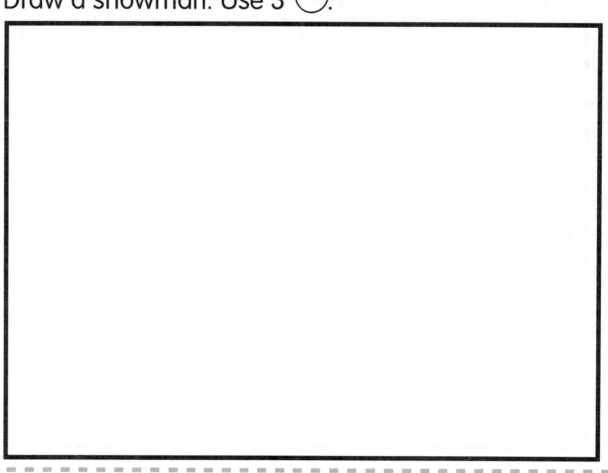

Drawing circles to make a picture

# Trace and write the numbers.

1

2

3

4

5

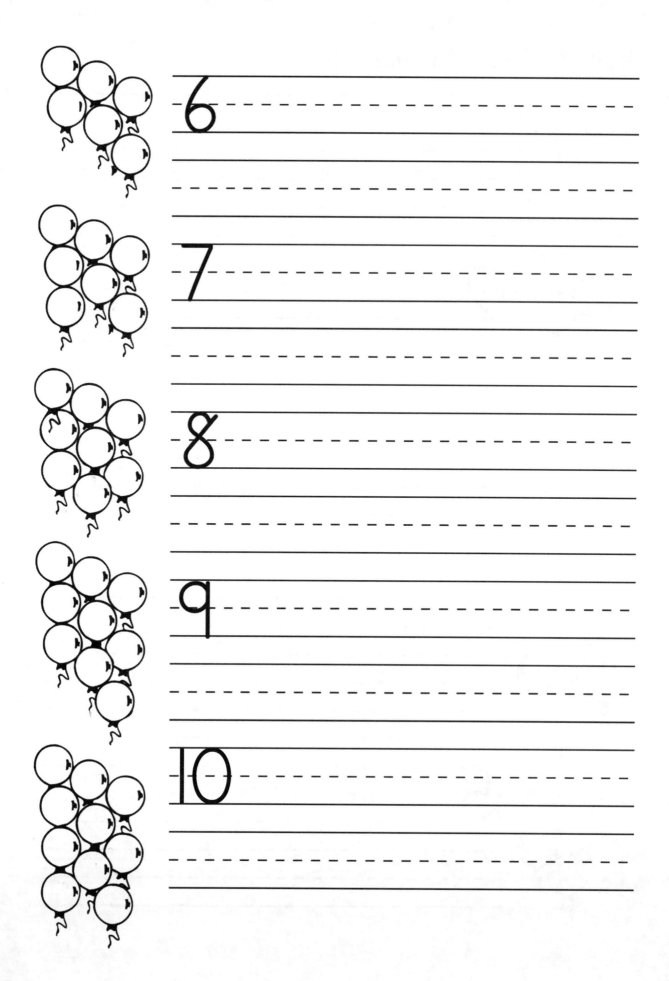

6

7

8

9

10

Tracing and writing numerals 6 to 10

# Count the flowers. Match them to the numbers.

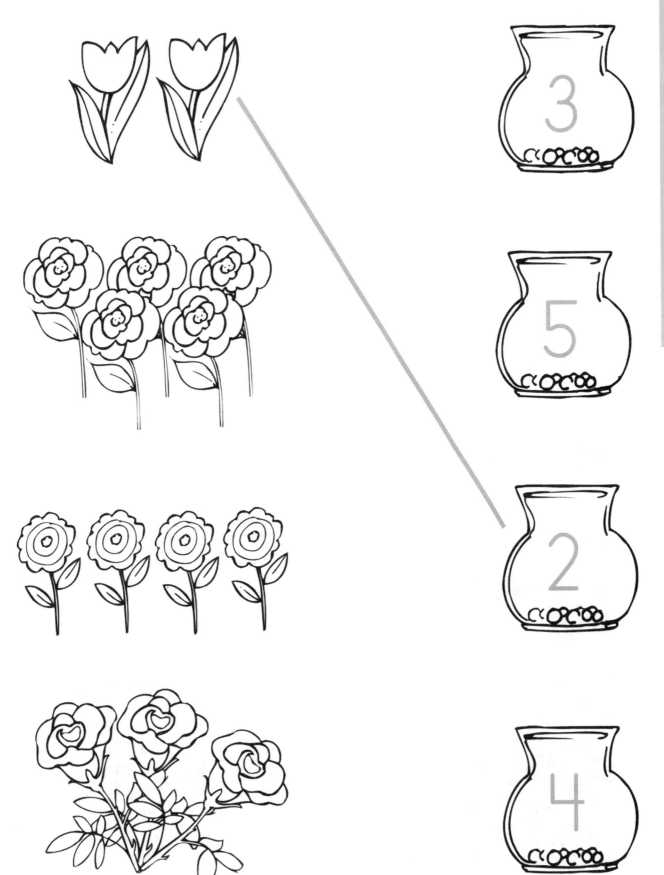

Counting; matching sets to numerals

# Count the fish. Match them to the numbers.

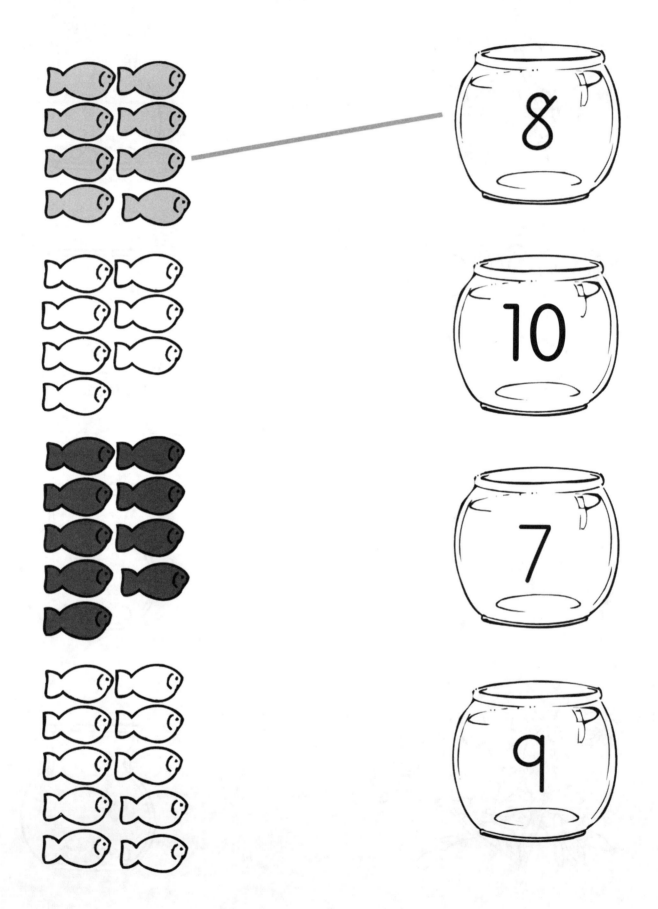

Counting; matching sets to numerals

# Circle the correct number.

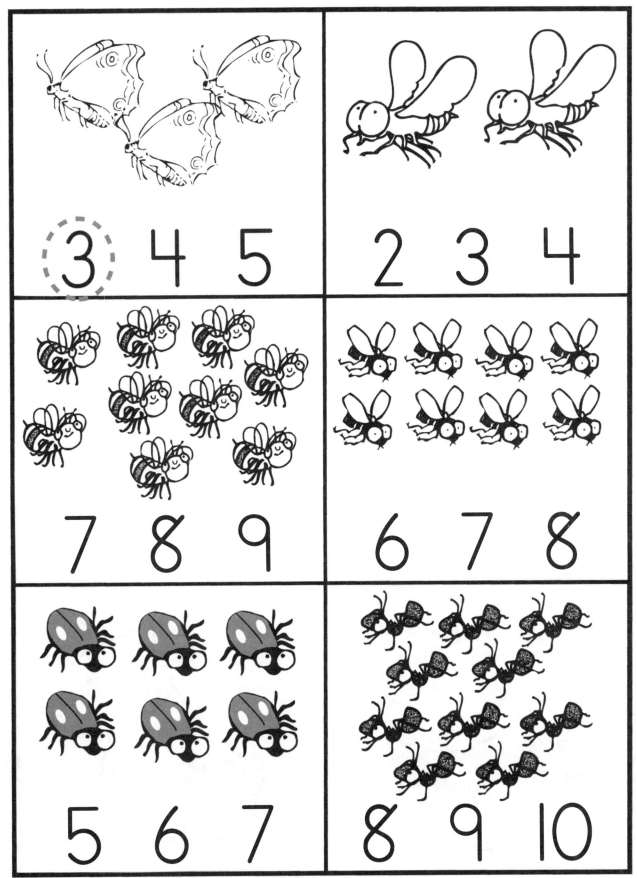

3   4   5

2   3   4

7   8   9

6   7   8

5   6   7

8   9   10

# Draw the correct number of spots on the pups.

Drawing a specified number of objects

# Color the things that rhyme.

Identifying objects whose names rhyme

# Match the things that rhyme.

Matching objects whose names rhyme

# Cut out the pictures.
# Paste them next to something that rhymes.

Identifying objects whose names rhyme

# Match the things that rhyme.

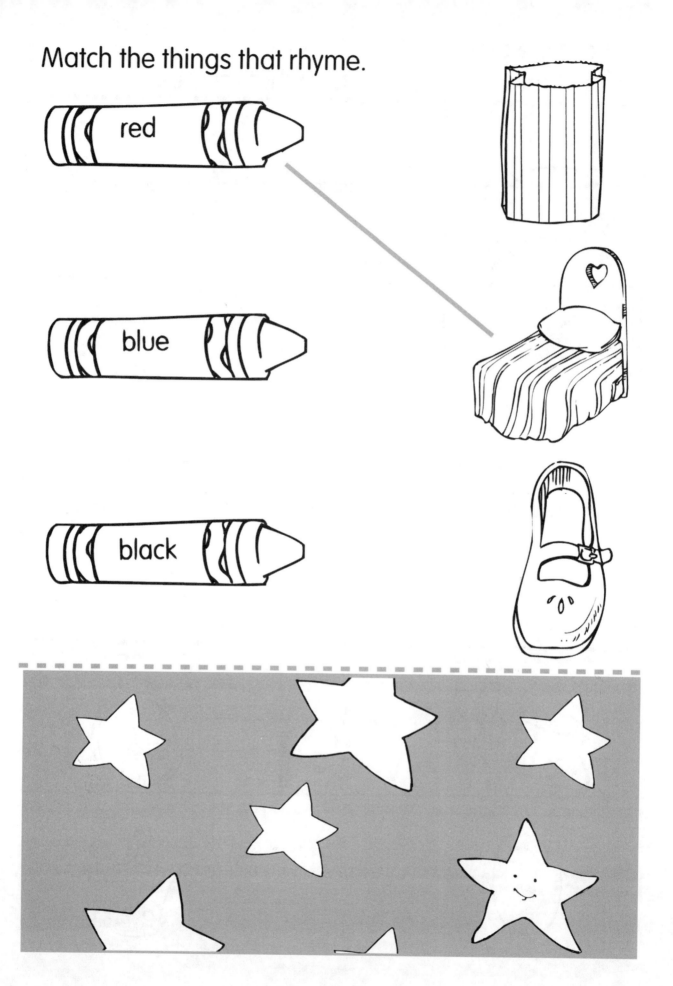

Matching rhyming words

# Color the shapes.

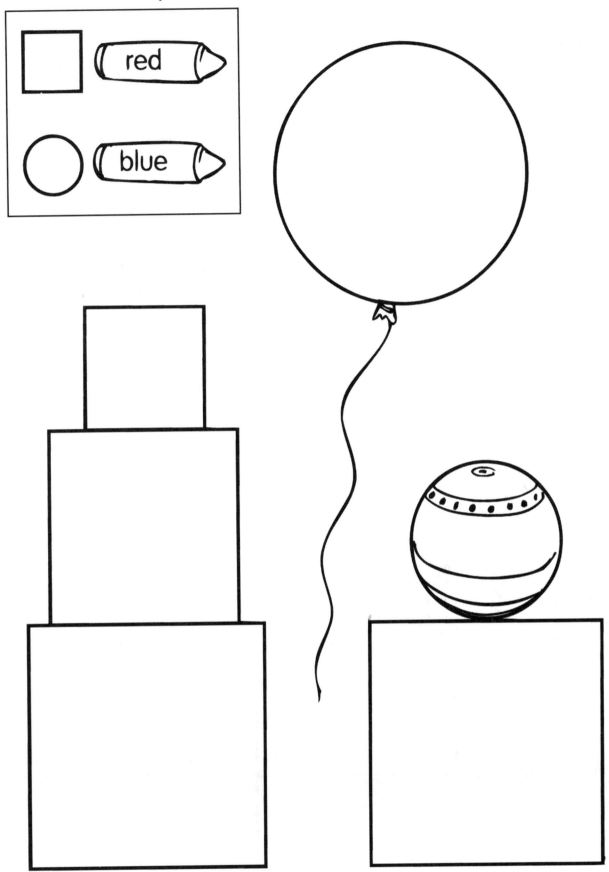

| | |
|---|---|
| ☐ | red |
| ○ | blue |

Recognizing shapes

# Color the shapes.

yellow

green

brown

Recognizing shapes

# Color the shapes.

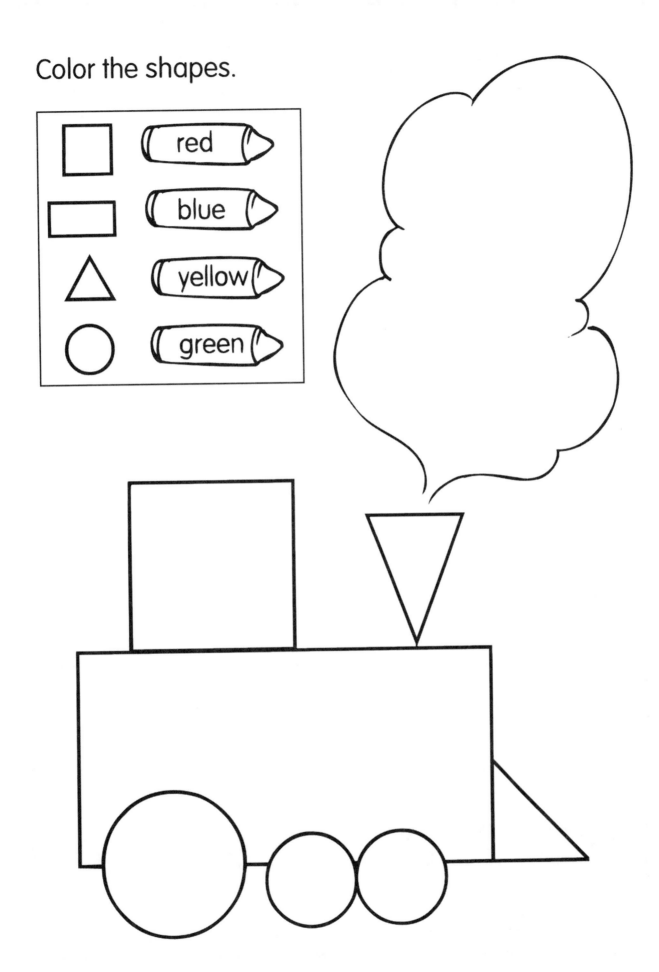

red

blue

yellow

green

# Trace and draw the shapes.

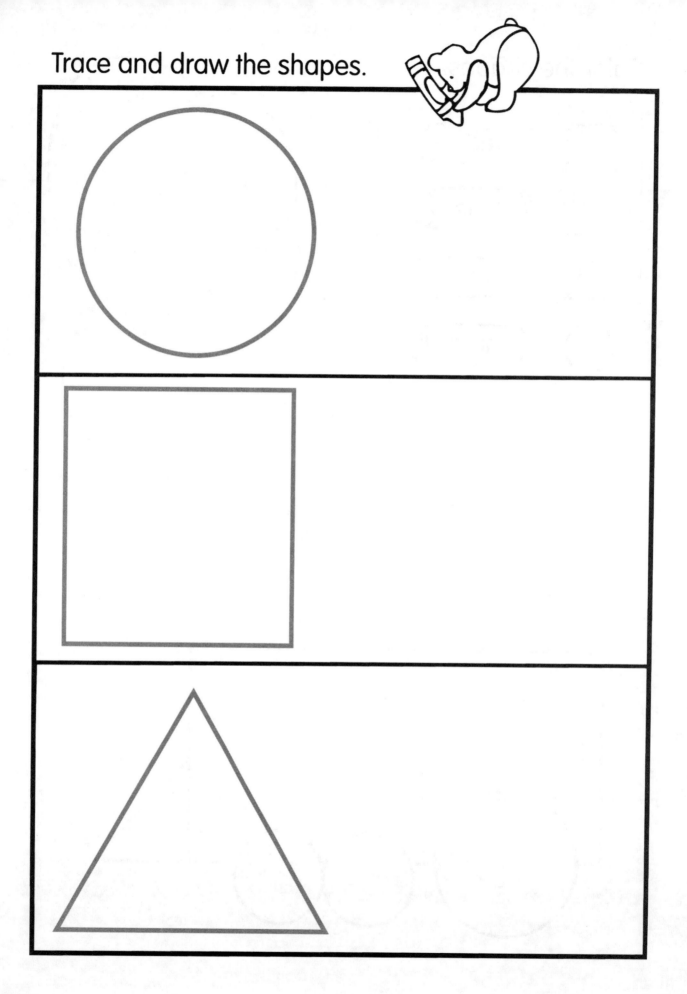

Tracing and drawing shapes

# Cut out the pictures.
# Paste them on the shapes.

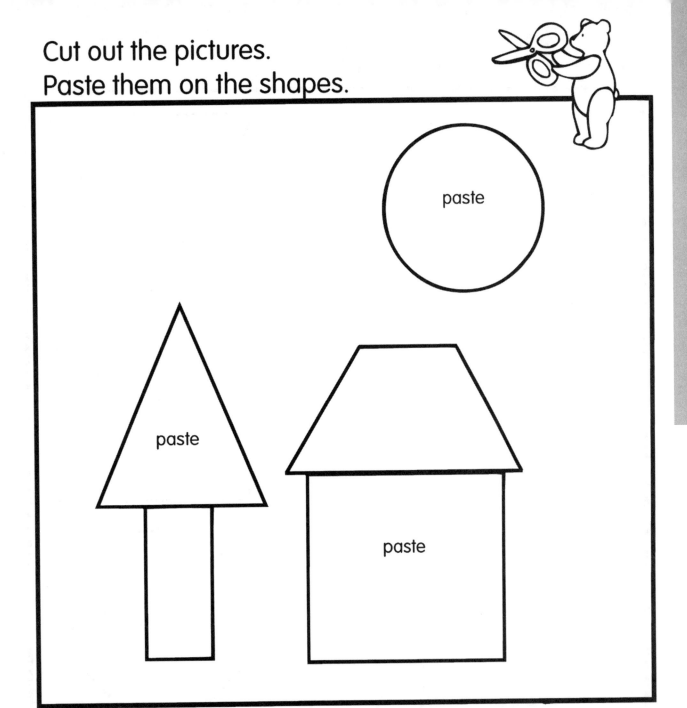

Matching shapes

# Match the shapes and color.

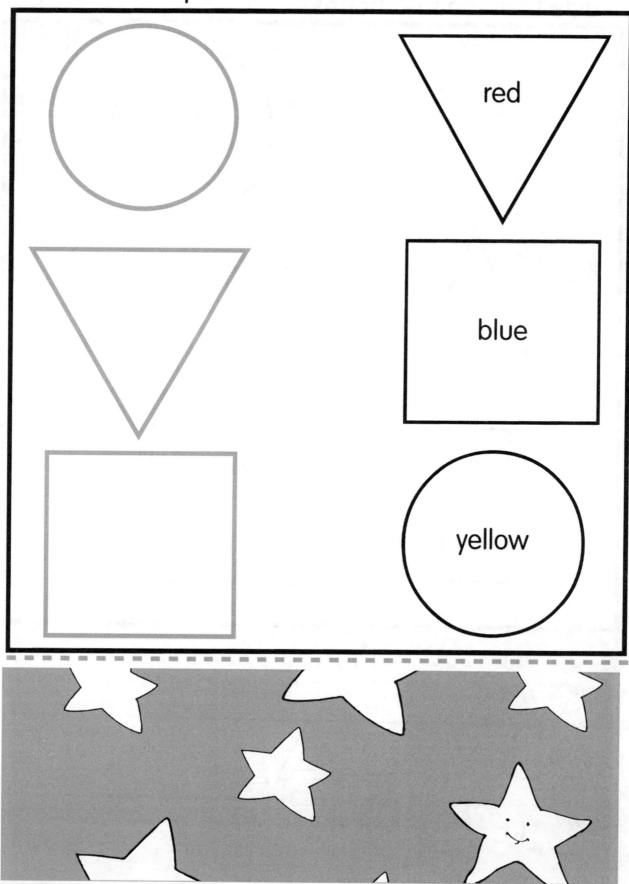

red

blue

yellow

Matching shapes

# Match the opposites.

# Match the opposites.

Matching opposites

# Cut out the pictures.
# Paste each picture by its opposite.

# Connect the dots and color.

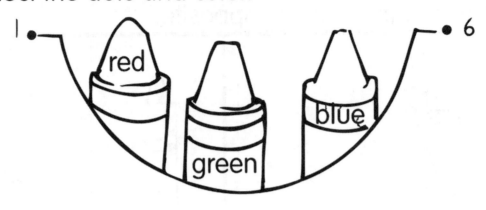

1 • red green blue • 6

## crayons

2 • yellow 5

orange

3 • • 4

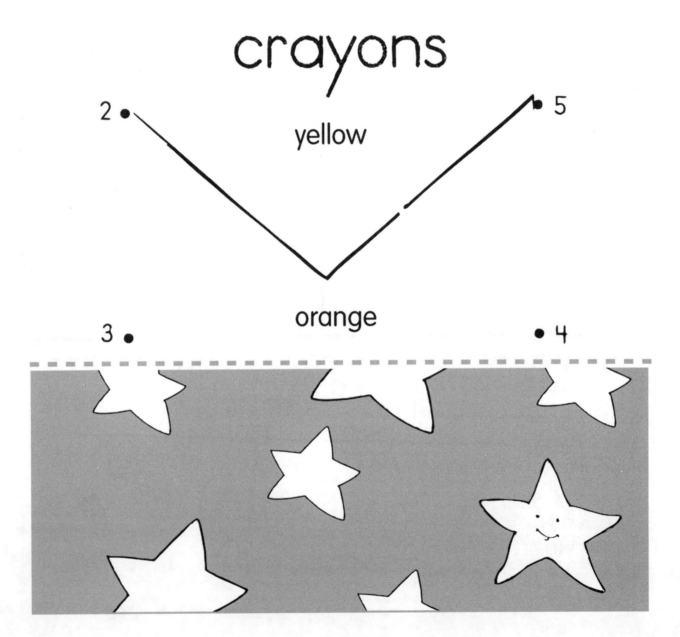

Understanding number order; recognizing color words

# Read the words. Color the picture.

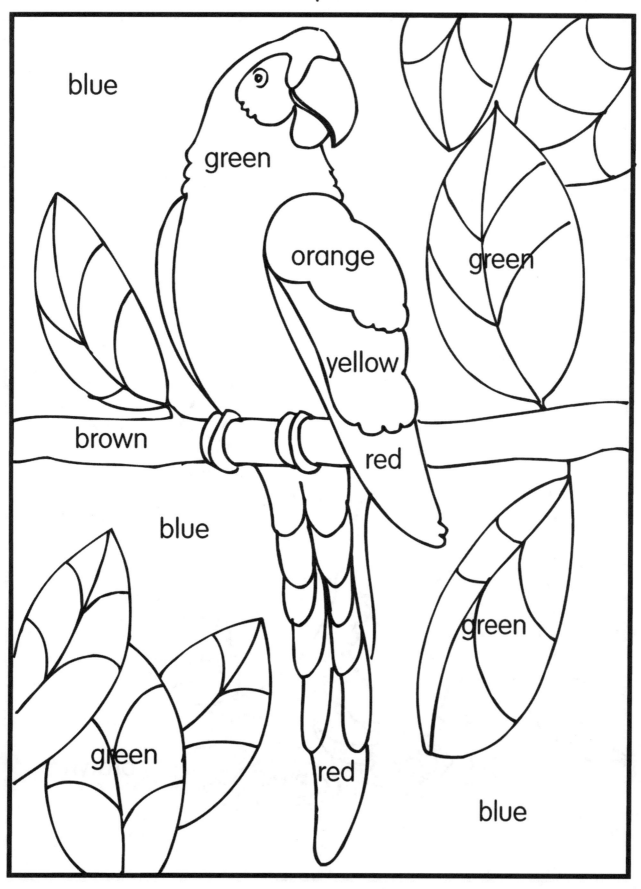

blue

green

orange

green

yellow

brown

red

blue

green

green

red

blue

Recognizing color words; following directions

# Read the words. Color the picture.

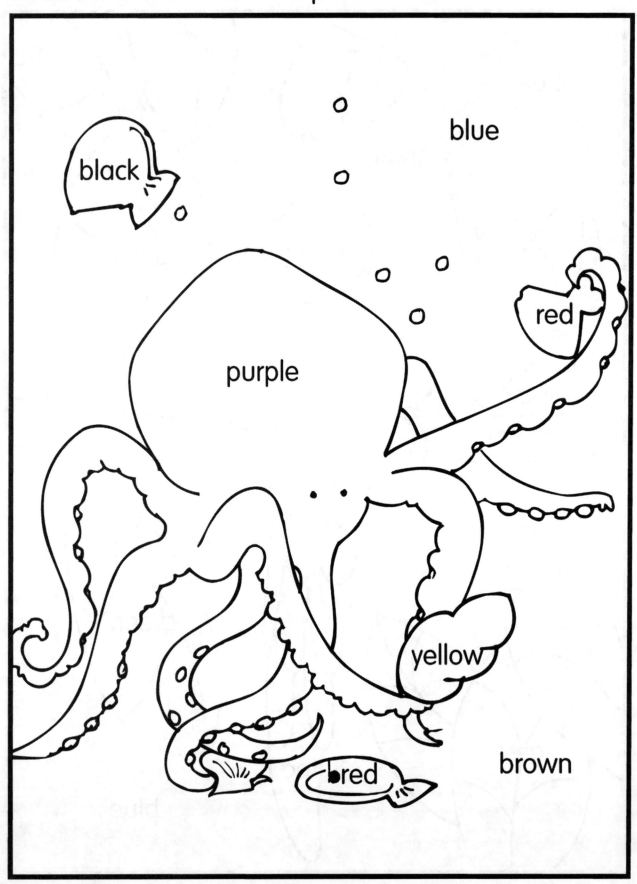

Recognizing color words; following directions

# Answer Key

Please take time to go over the work your child has completed. Ask your child to explain what he/she has done. Praise both success and effort. If mistakes have been made, explain what the answer should have been and how to find it. Let your child know that mistakes are a part of learning. The time you spend with your child helps let him/her know you feel learning is important.

Getting Ready for Preschool and Kindergarten

page 11

page 12

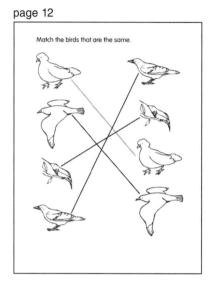

page 13

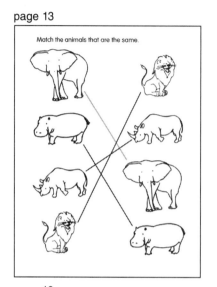

page 14

page 15

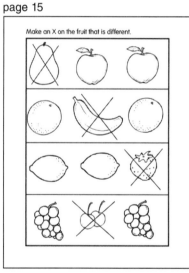

page 16

page 17

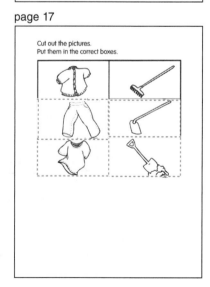

page 19

page 21

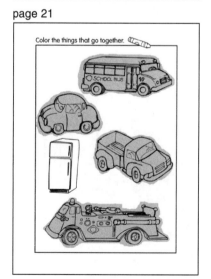

**page 22**

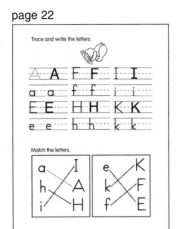

**page 23**

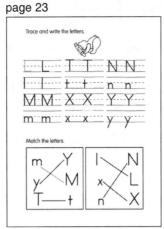

**page 24**

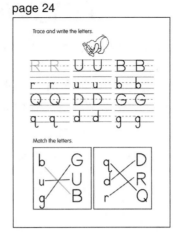

**page 25**

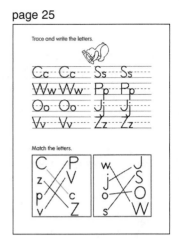

**page 26**

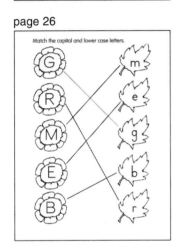

**page 27**

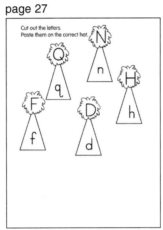

**page 31**

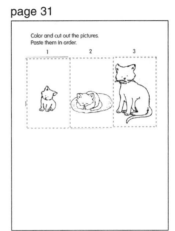

**page 33**

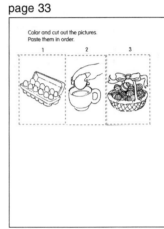

**page 34**

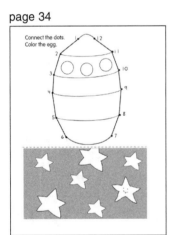

**page 35**

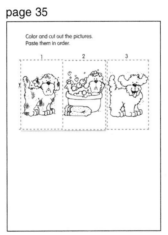

**page 36**

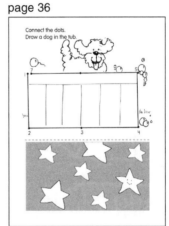

**page 37**

**page 38**

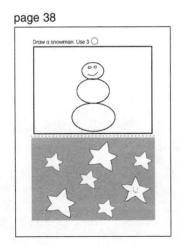

**page 41**

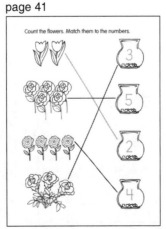

**page 42**

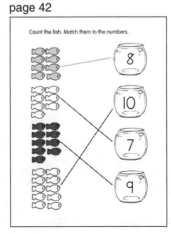

**page 43**

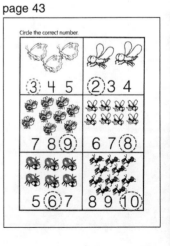

Answers

**page 44**

Draw the correct number of spots on the pups.

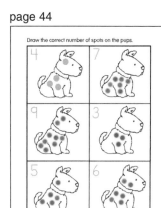

**page 45**

Color the things that rhyme.

**page 46**

Match the things that rhyme.

**page 47**

Cut out the pictures.
Paste them next to something that rhymes.

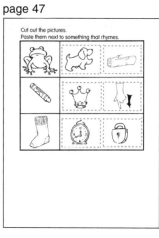

**page 48**

Match the things that rhyme.

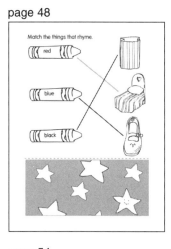

**page 49**

Color the shapes.

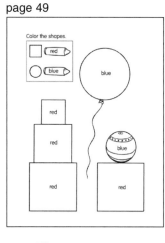

**page 50**

Color the shapes.

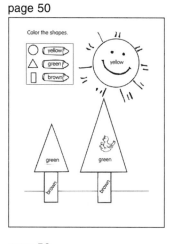

**page 51**

Color the shapes.

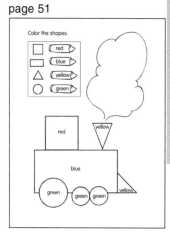

**page 54**

Match the shapes and color.

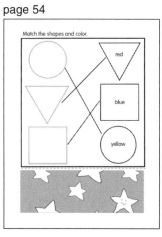

**page 55**

Match the opposites.

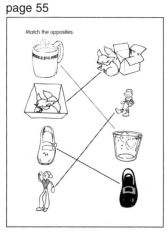

**page 56**

Match the opposites.

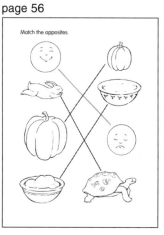

**page 57**

Cut out the pictures.
Paste each picture by its opposite.

**page 58**

Connect the dots and color.

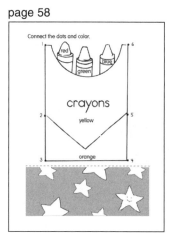

Answers

# Trace and write.

A A A A A

a a a a a

Tracing and writing capital and lowercase: Aa

# Color.

A ( brown )
a ( yellow )

# Trace and write.

B B B B B

b b b b b

Tracing and writing capital and lowercase: Bb

# What is hiding here?

B (orange)   b (black)   A (blue)

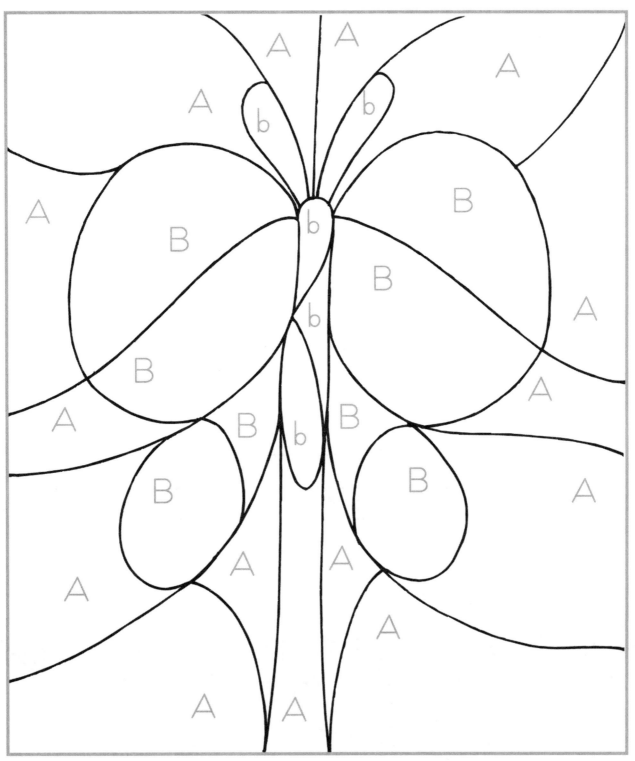

Distinguishing between capital and lowercase: Bb, A

# Trace and write.

C C C C C

c c c c c

Tracing and writing capital and lowercase: Cc

# What is hiding here?

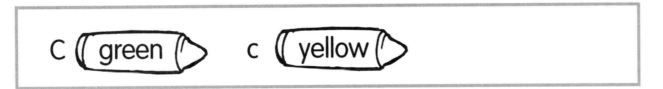

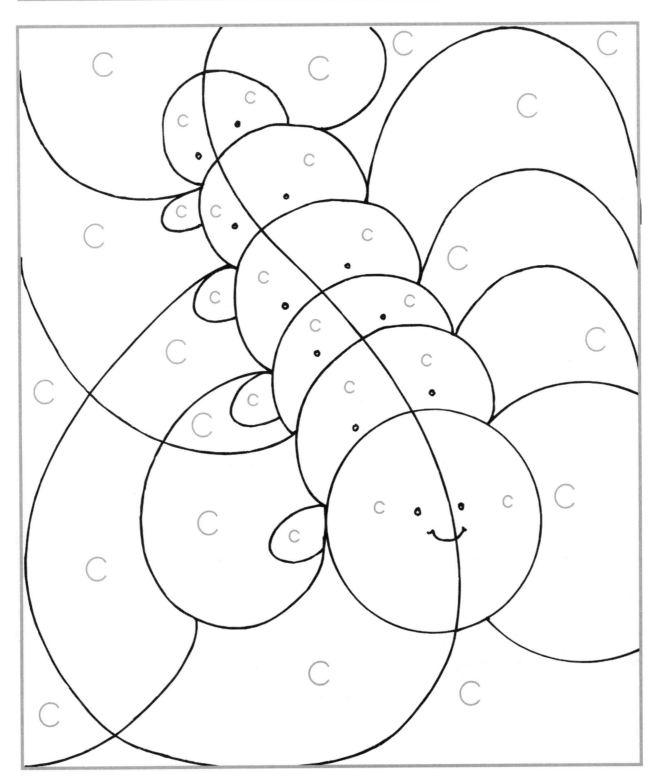

# Trace and write.

D D D D D

d d d d d

Tracing and writing capital and lowercase: Dd

# Color.

D [ blue ]   d [ orange ]

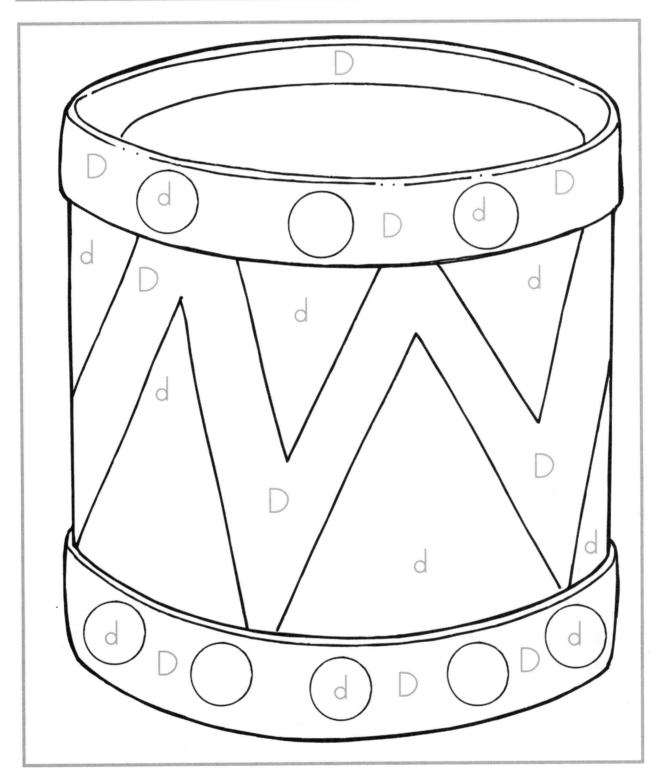

Distinguishing between capital and lowercase: Dd    71

# Trace and write.

E E E E E

e e e e e

Tracing and writing capital and lowercase: Ee

# Color.

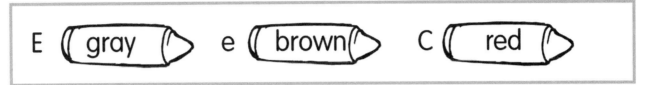

E ⟨ gray ⟩   e ⟨ brown ⟩   C ⟨ red ⟩

Distinguishing between capital and lowercase: Ee, C

# Trace and write.

FFFFF

fffff

Tracing and writing capital and lowercase: Ff

# What is hiding here?

F (brown)    f (green)    E (blue)

# Match 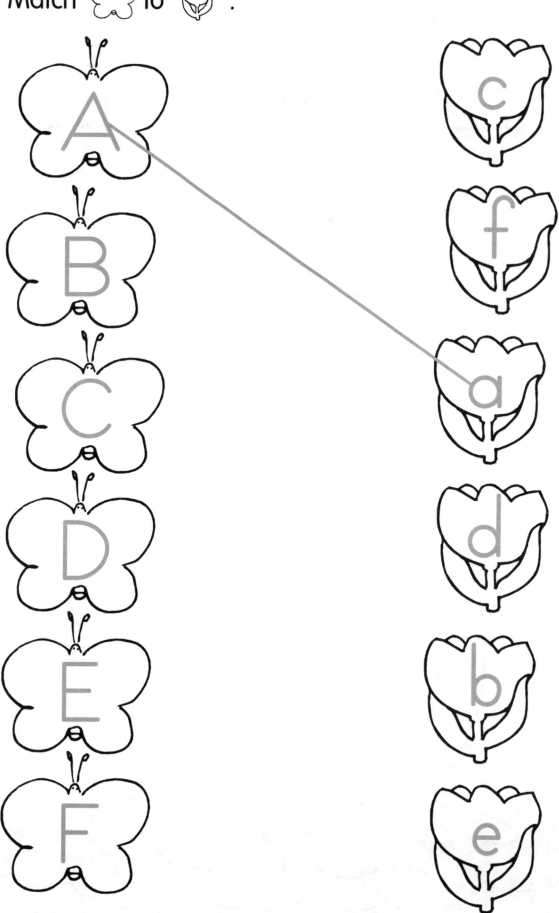 to .

Matching capital and lowercase letters: Aa to Ff

# Trace and write.

bed          beads          bag

# Trace and write.

G G G G G

g g g g g

Tracing and writing capital and lowercase: Gg

# Color.

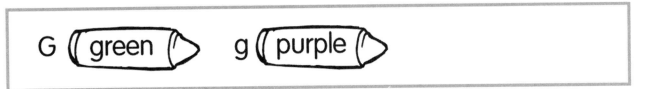

G ( green )   g ( purple )

Distinguishing between capital and lowercase: Gg

# Trace and write.

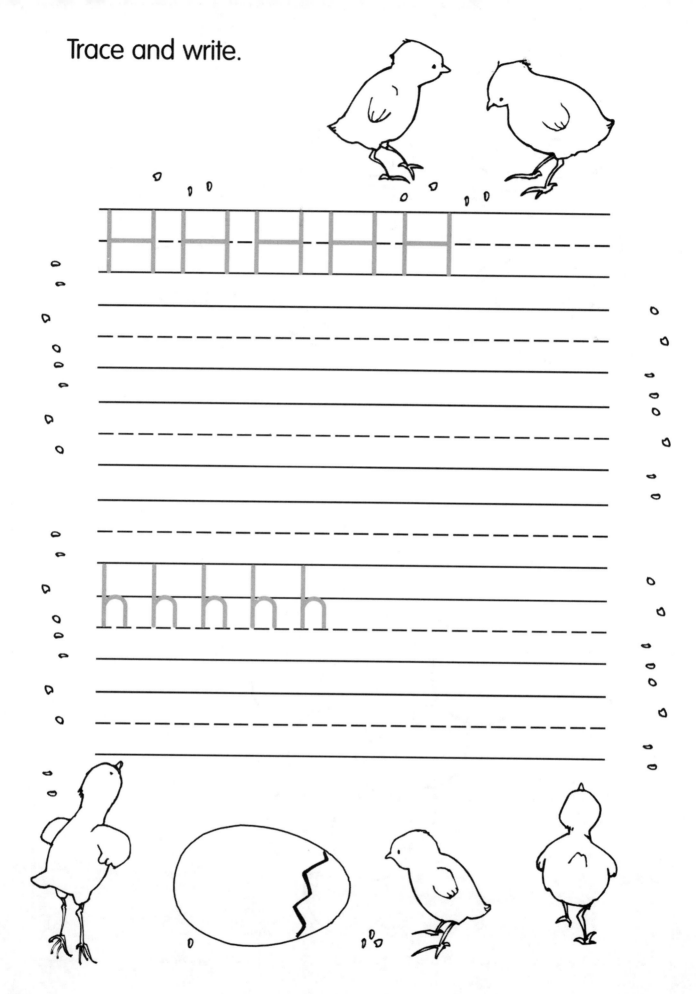

Tracing and writing capital and lowercase: Hh

# Color.

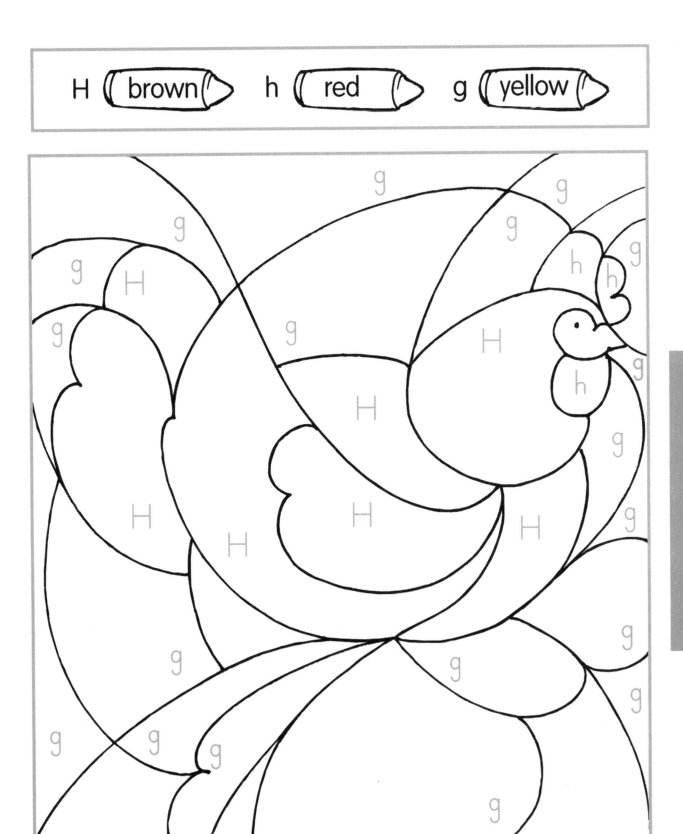

Learning the Letters of the Alphabet

# Trace and write.

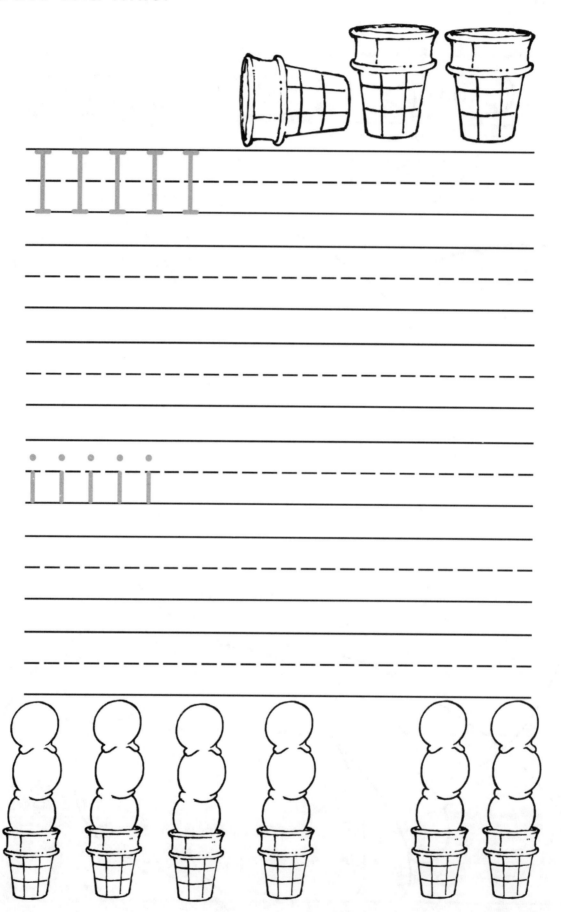

Tracing and writing capital and lowercase: Ii

# Color.

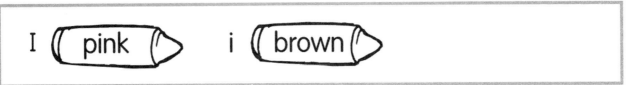

I ⬤ pink        i ⬤ brown

Distinguishing between capital and lowercase: Ii

# Trace and write.

J J J J J

j j j j j

Tracing and writing capital and lowercase: Jj

# Color.

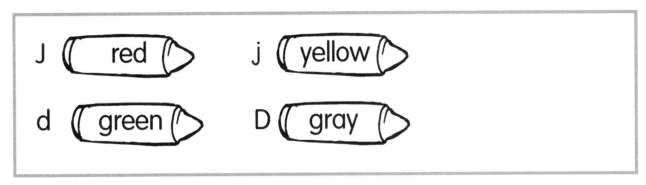

J ( red )    j ( yellow )

d ( green )    D ( gray )

Learning the Letters of the Alphabet

# Trace and write.

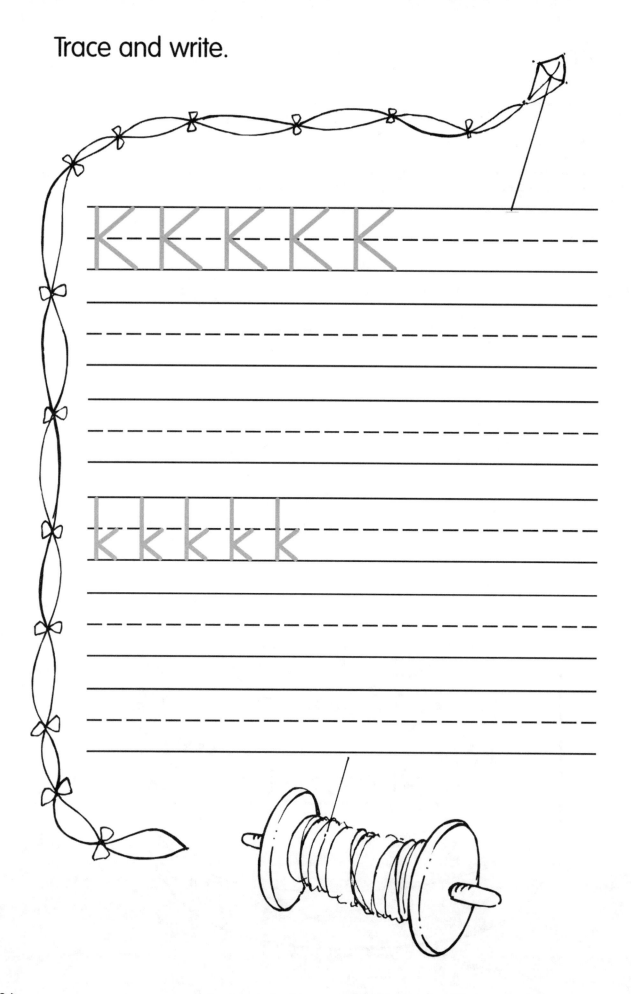

K K K K

k k k k

Tracing and writing capital and lowercase: Kk

# What is hiding here?

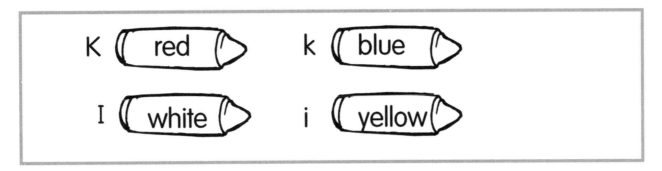

Distinguishing between capital and lowercase: Kk, Ii

# Trace and write.

Tracing and writing capital and lowercase: Ll

# Color.

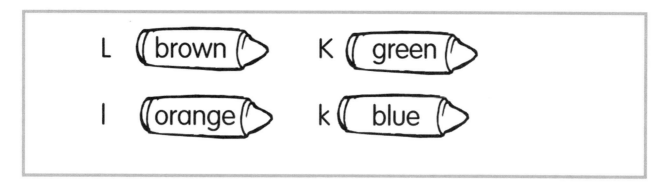

L  brown      K  green

l  orange     k  blue

Distinguishing between capital and lowercase: Ll, Kk

Match 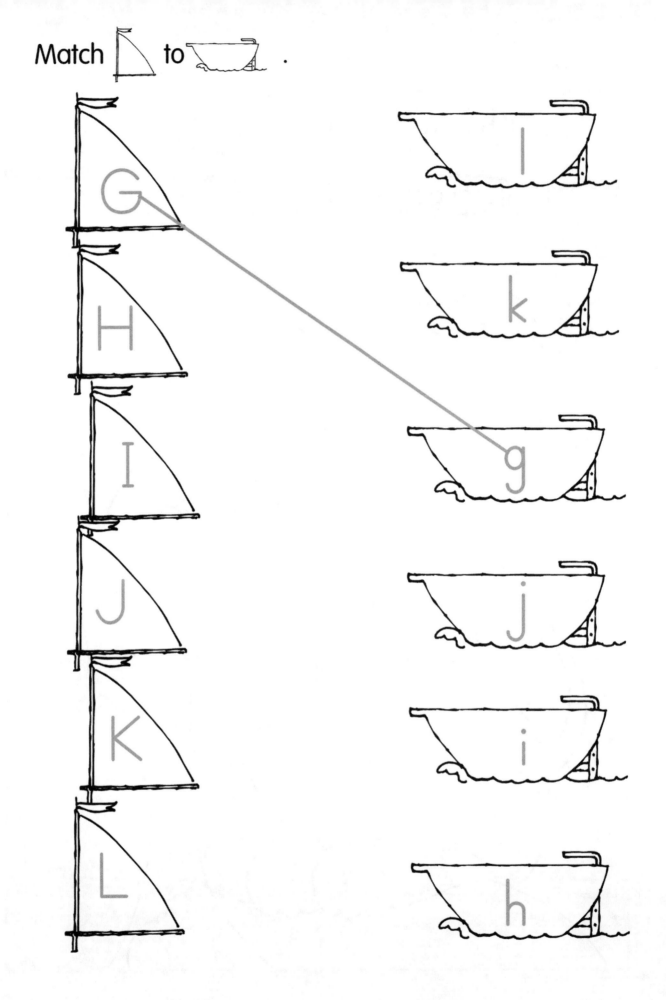 to .

Matching capital and lowercase letters: Gg to Ll

# Trace and write.

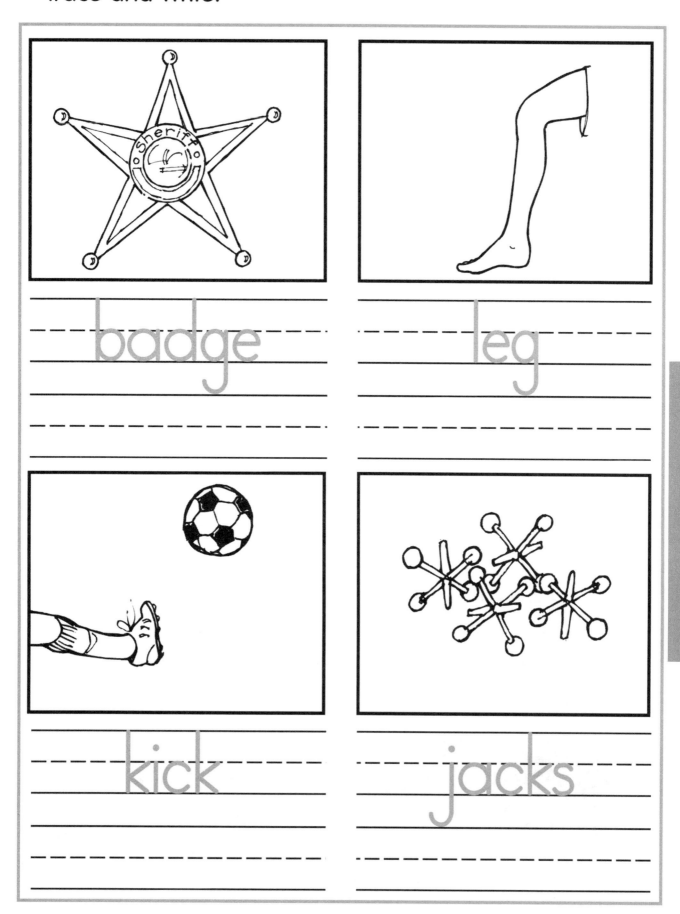

badge

leg

kick

jacks

# Trace and write.

M M M M M

m m m m m

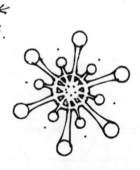

Tracing and writing capital and lowercase: Mm

# What is hiding here?

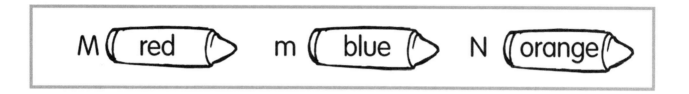

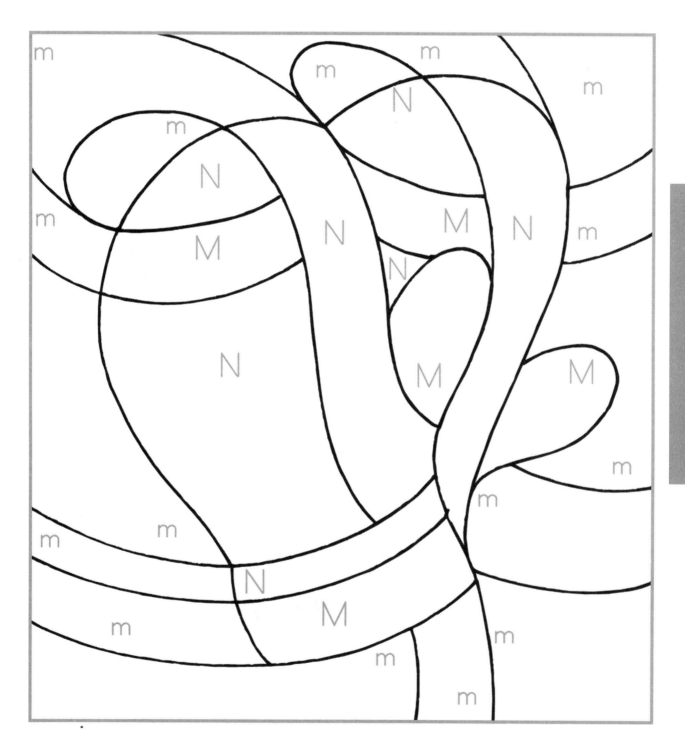

Distinguishing between capital and lowercase: Mm, N

# Trace and write.

NNNNN

N

N

nnnnn

n

n

Tracing and writing capital and lowercase: Nn

# What is hiding here?

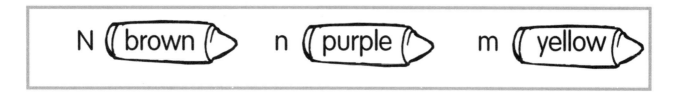

N ( brown )  n ( purple )  m ( yellow )

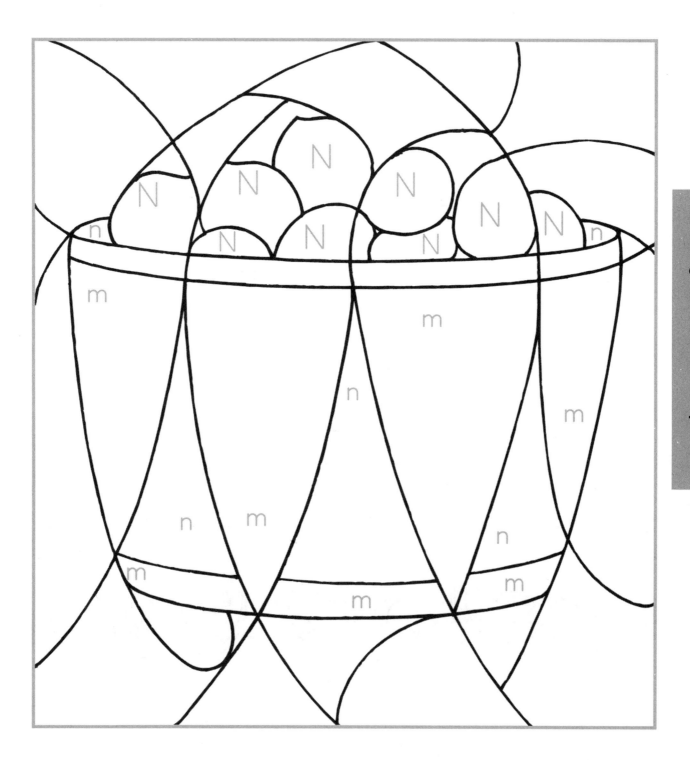

Distinguishing between capital and lowercase: Nn, m

# Trace and write.

O O O O O

o o o o o

Tracing and writing capital and lowercase: Oo

# Color.

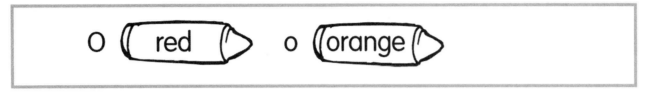

O red     o orange

Learning the Letters of the Alphabet

# Trace and write.

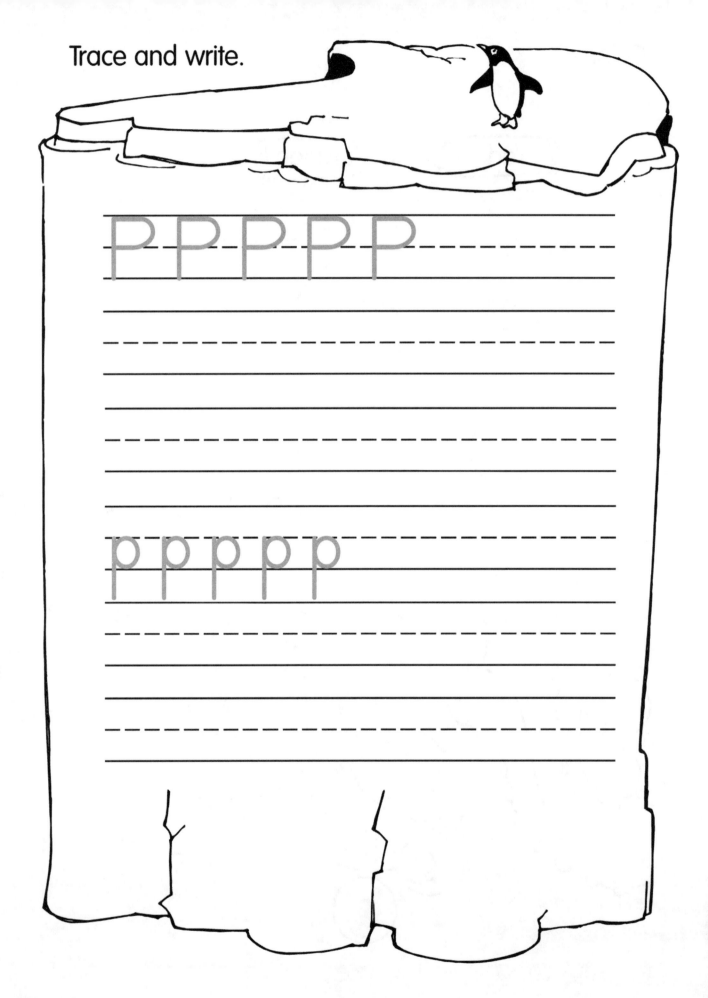

P P P P

p p p p

Tracing and writing capital and lowercase: Pp

# What is hiding here?

P ( black )   p ( white )   g ( blue )

Distinguishing between capital and lowercase: Pp, g

# Trace and write.

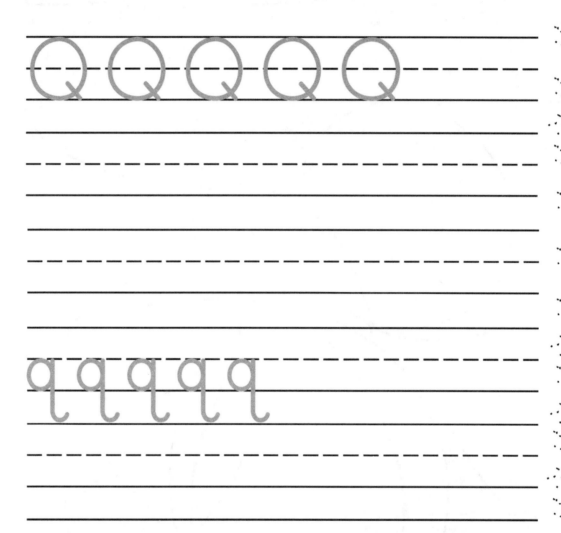

Tracing and writing capital and lowercase: Qq

# Color.

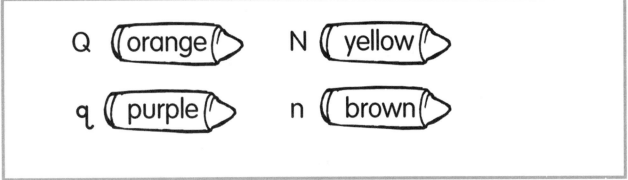

Q (orange)    N (yellow)

q (purple)    n (brown)

# Trace and write.

RRRRR

rrrrr

Tracing and writing capital and lowercase: Rr

# Color.

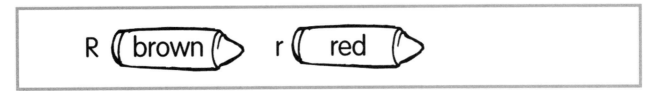

R ( brown )    r ( red )

Match  to 🌨 .

Matching capital and lowercase letters: Mm to Rr

# Trace and write.

lamb    pail    orange

Tracing and writing words using lowercase letters

# Trace and write.

S S S S S

S S S S S

Tracing and writing capital and lowercase: Ss

# What is hiding here?

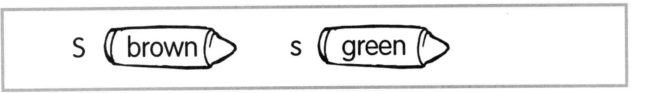

S ⟨brown⟩    s ⟨green⟩

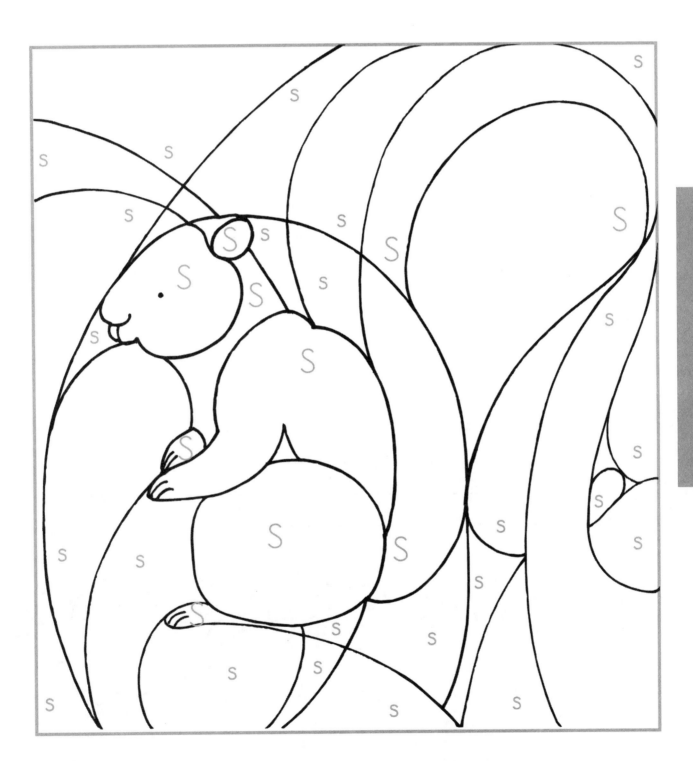

Distinguishing between capital and lowercase: Ss

# Trace and write.

T T T T T

t t t t t

Tracing and writing capital and lowercase: Tt

# Color.

T green    t brown

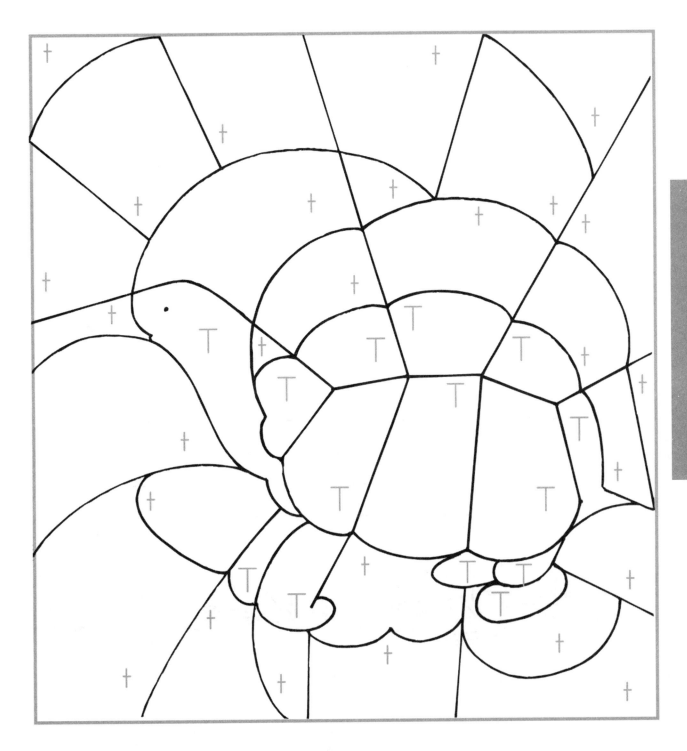

Distinguishing between capital and lowercase: Tt

# Trace and write.

UUUUU

uuuuu

Tracing and writing capital and lowercase: Uu

# Color.

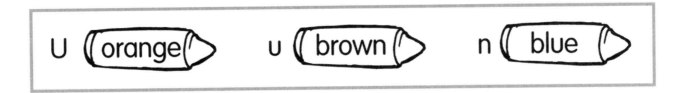

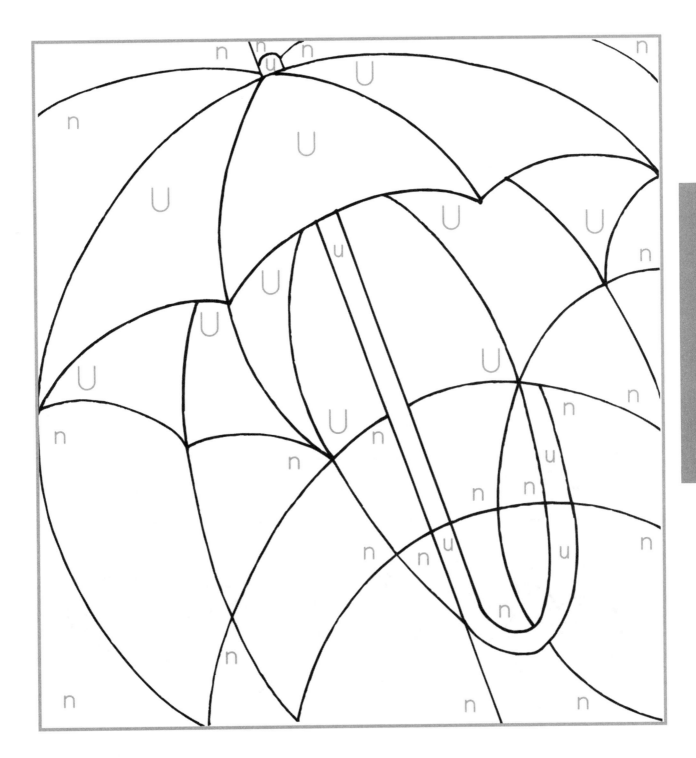

Distinguishing between capital and lowercase: Uu, n

# Trace and write.

VVVVV

VVVVV

Tracing and writing capital and lowercase: Vv

# What is hiding here?

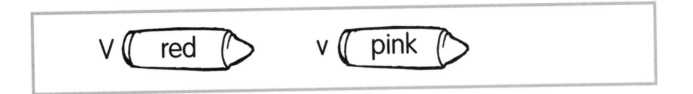

V red     v pink

# Trace and write.

WWWWW

wwwww

Tracing and writing capital and lowercase: Ww

# What is hiding here?

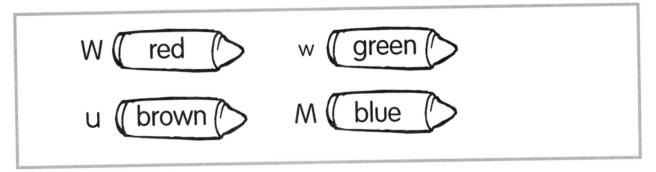

W ( red )   w ( green )

u ( brown )   M ( blue )

Distinguishing between capital and lowercase: Ww, u, M

115

# Trace and write.

Tracing and writing capital and lowercase: Xx

# Color.

X ( orange )    x ( brown )

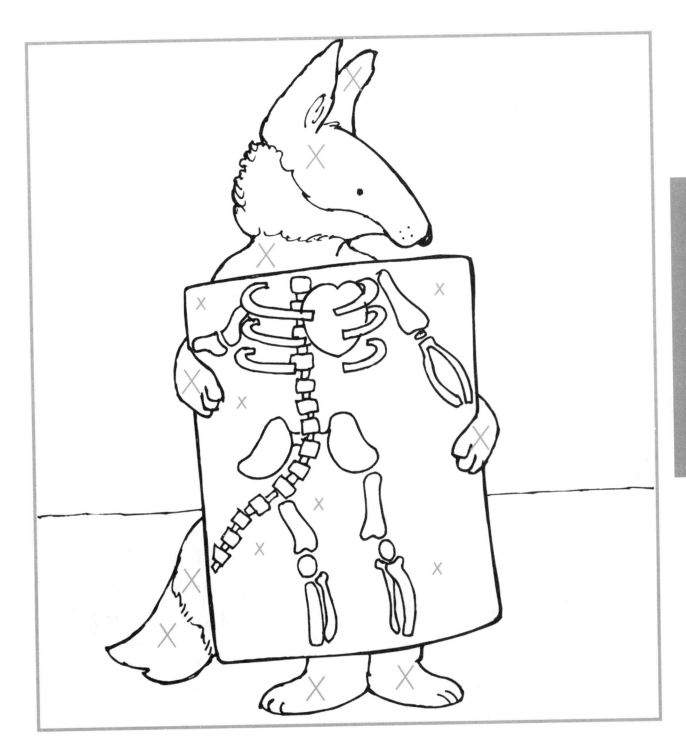

# Trace and write.

Y Y Y Y Y

y y y y y

Tracing and writing capital and lowercase: Yy

# What is hiding here?

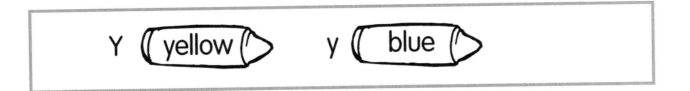

Y (yellow)     y (blue)

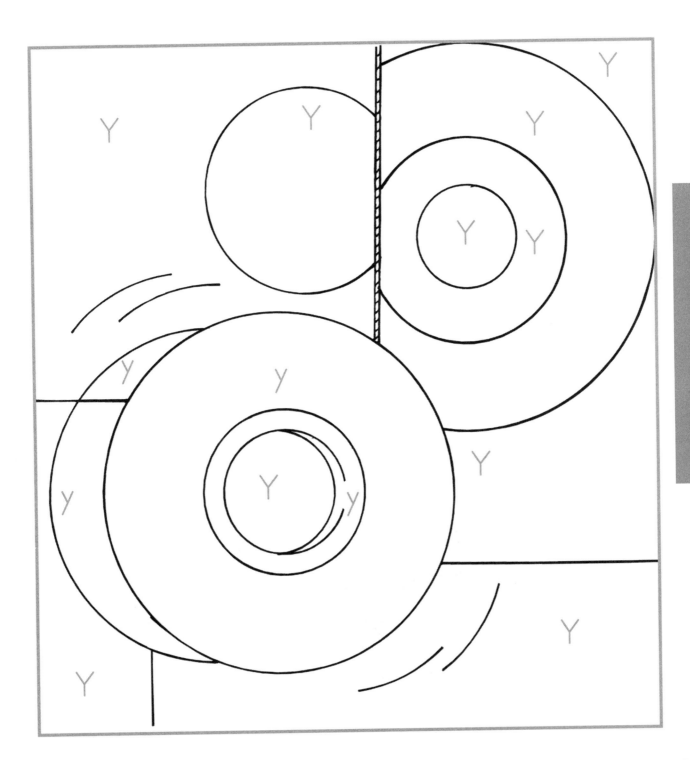

Distinguishing between capital and lowercase: Yy     **119**

# Trace and write.

ZZZZZ

zzzzz

Tracing and writing capital and lowercase: Zz

# Color.

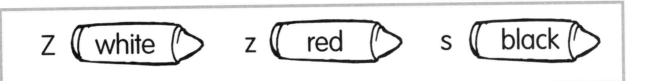

Z white   z red   s black

Distinguishing between capital and lowercase: Zz, s

# Match.

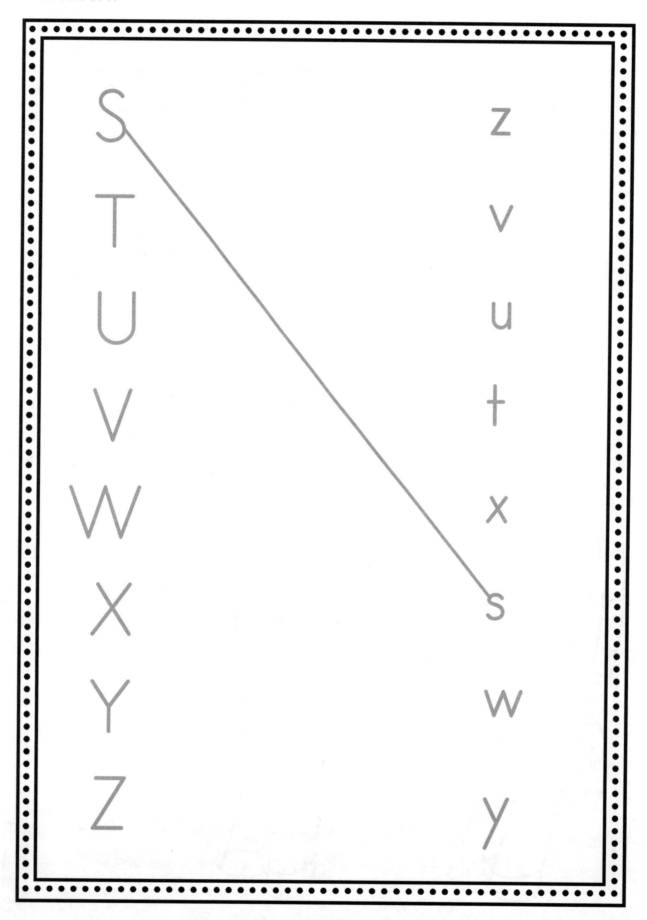

Matching capital and lowercase letters: Ss to Zz

# Copy the words.

smile

ship

watch

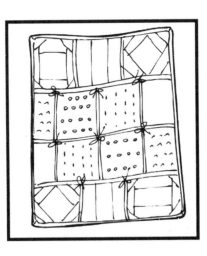

chair

zebra

quilt

# The Alphabet

## Uppercase Letters

A B C D E F G
H I J K L M N
O P Q R S T U
V W X Y Z

## Lowercase Letters

a b c d e f g
h i j k l m n
o p q r s t u
v w x y z

Writing capital and lowercase letters

# Answer Key

Please take time to go over the work your child has completed. Ask your child to explain what he/she has done. Praise both success and effort. If mistakes have been made, explain what the answer should have been and how to find it. Let your child know that mistakes are a part of learning. The time you spend with your child helps let him/her know you feel learning is important.

page 65

page 67

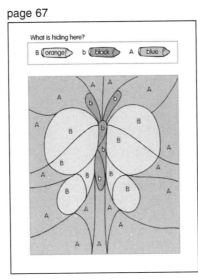

page 69

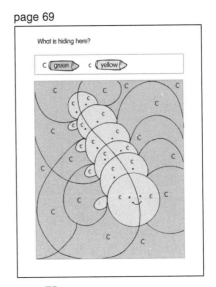

page 71

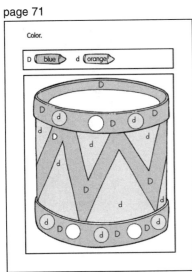

page 73

page 75

page 76

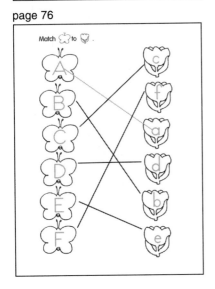

page 79

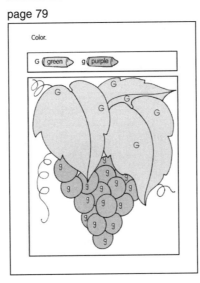

page 81

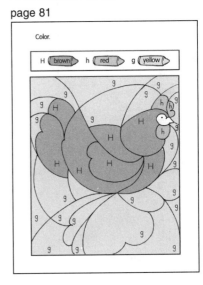

### page 83

Color.

I ( pink )   i ( brown )

### page 85

Color.

J ( red )   J ( yellow )
d ( green )   D ( gray )

Strawberry Jam

### page 87

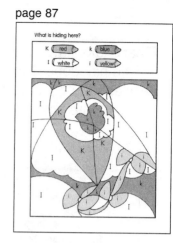

What is hiding here?

K ( red )   k ( blue )
I ( white )   i ( yellow )

### page 89

Color.

L ( brown )   K ( green )
I ( orange )   k ( blue )

### page 90

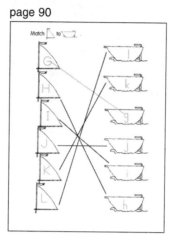

Match ◢ to ◡ .

G
H
I
J
K
L

### page 93

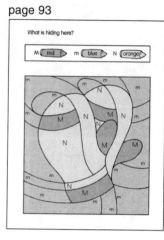

What is hiding here?

M ( red )   m ( blue )   N ( orange )

### page 95

What is hiding here?

N ( brown )   n ( purple )   m ( yellow )

### page 97

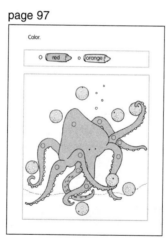

Color.

O ( red )   o ( orange )

### page 99

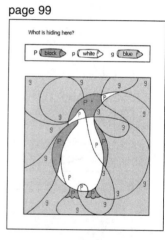

What is hiding here?

P ( black )   p ( white )   g ( blue )

### page 101

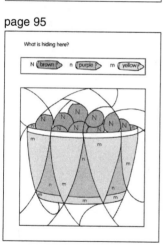

Color.

Q ( orange )   N ( yellow )
q ( purple )   n ( brown )

### page 103

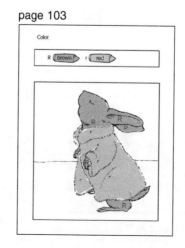

Color.

R ( brown )   r ( red )

### page 104

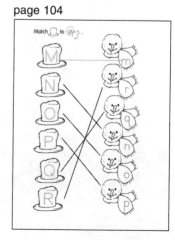

Match 🎩 to ☃ .

M
N
O
P
Q
R

m
r
q
n
o
p

126

Answers

page 107

What is hiding here?

S ( brown )   s ( green )

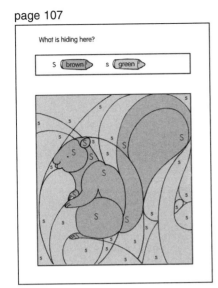

page 109

Color.

T ( green )   t ( brown )

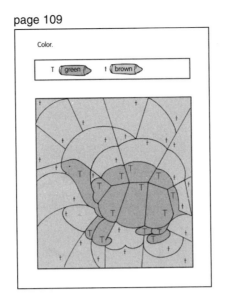

page 111

Color.

U ( orange )   u ( brown )   n ( blue )

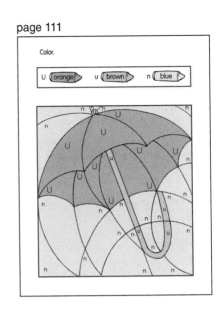

page 113

What is hiding here?

V ( red )   v ( pink )

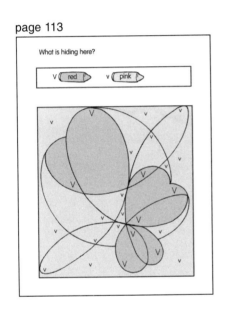

page 115

What is hiding here?

W ( red )   w ( green )
u ( brown )   M ( blue )

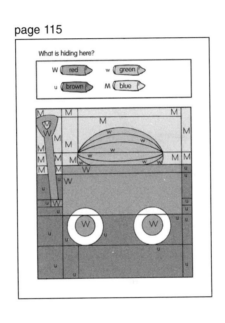

page 117

Color.

X ( orange )   x ( brown )

page 119

What is hiding here?

Y ( yellow )   y ( blue )

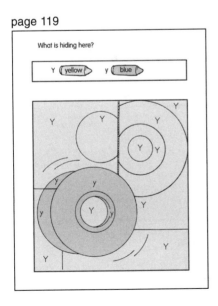

page 121

Color.

Z ( white )   z ( red )   s ( black )

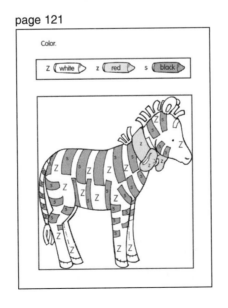

page 122

Match.

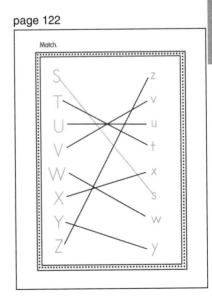

# Aa

# astronaut

Recognizing the letter Aa; associating the short a sound with the letter

# What begins with the sound made by the letter A?

Identifying objects whose names begin with the sound of short a

Alphabet Sounds

# Bb

# bear

Recognizing the letter Bb; associating a sound with the letter

# What begins with the sound made by the letter B?

Alphabet Sounds

Cc

cake

Recognizing the letter Cc; associating a sound with the letter

# What begins with the sound made by the letter C?

Identifying objects whose names begin with the sound associated with the letter c

**Dd**

**dog**

Recognizing the letter Dd; associating a sound with the letter

# What begins with the sound made by the letter D?

Alphabet Sounds

Note: Point to the letter and ask your child to name it. Tell the name if it is unknown to your child. Next ask for the name of the picture and the sound heard at the begining of the word.

**E e**

## elephant

Recognizing the letter Ee; associating the short e sound with the letter

# What begins with the sound made by the letter E?

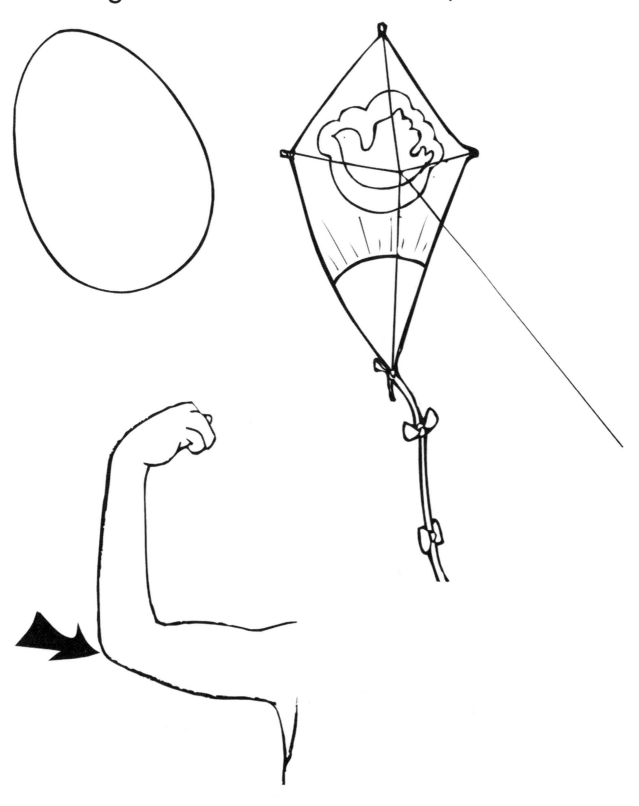

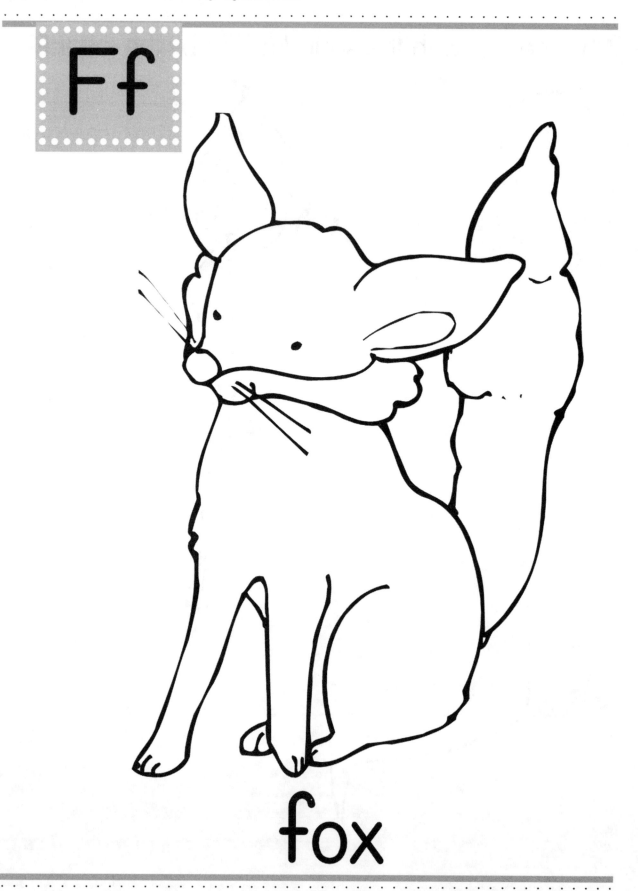

fox

Recognizing the letter Ff; associating a sound with the letter

# What begins with the sound made by the letter F?

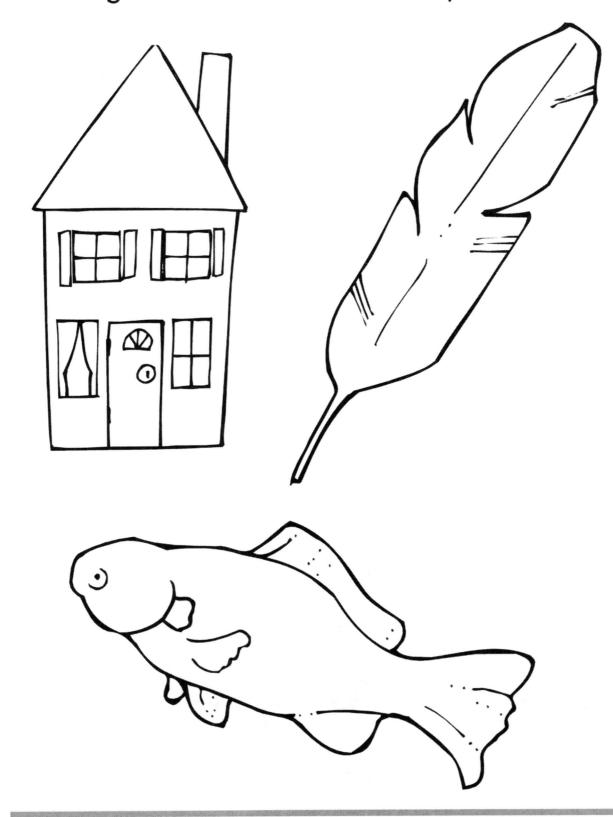

Alphabet Sounds

*Identifying objects whose names begin with the sound associated with the letter f*

**Gg**

# gorilla

Recognizing the letter Gg; associating a sound with the letter

# What begins with the sound made by the letter G?

Alphabet Sounds

Identifying objects whose names begin with the sound associated with the letter g

# Match.

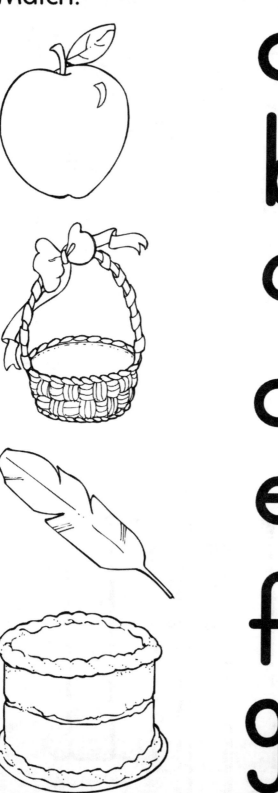

a

b

c

d

e

f

g

Matching letters with objects whose names begin with sounds associated with them

## Match.

A                   c

B

C                   b

D                   a

E                   e

F                   d

G                   g

                          f

Note: Point to the letter and ask your child to name it. Tell the name if it is unknown to your child. Next ask for the name of the picture and the sound heard at the begining of the word.

house

Recognizing the letter Hh; associating a sound with the letter

# What begins with the sound made by the letter H?

Identifying objects whose names begin with the sound associated with the letter h

# I i

# iguana

146        Recognizing the letter Ii; associating the short i sound with the letter

# What begins with the sound made by the letter I?

Alphabet Sounds

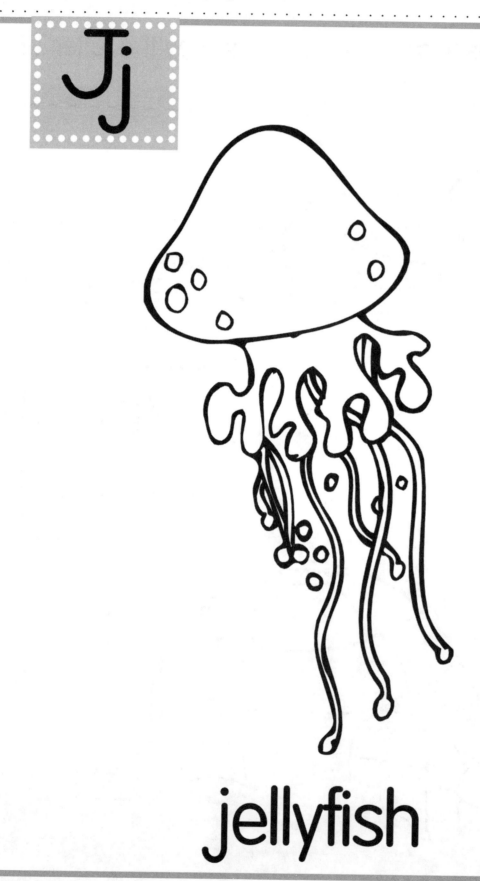

**J j**

# jellyfish

Recognizing the letter Jj; associating a sound with the letter

# What begins with the sound made by the letter J?

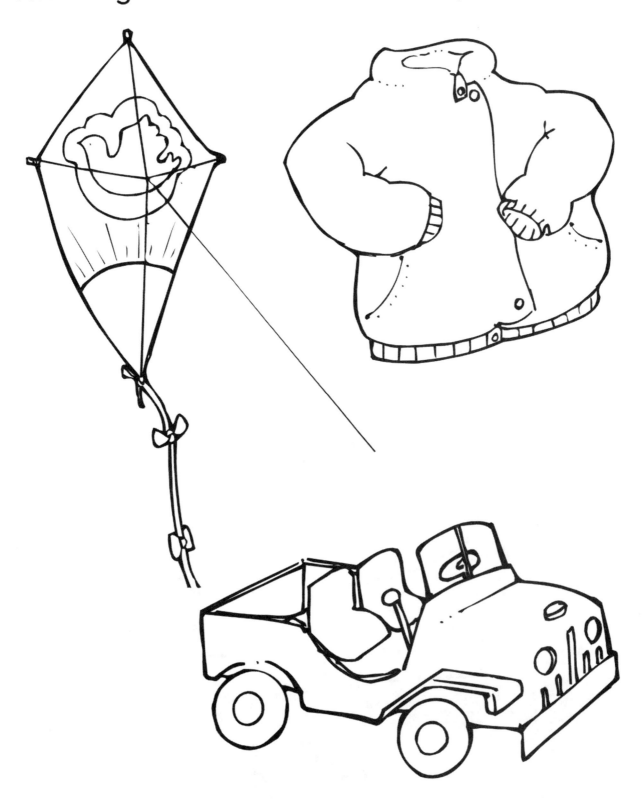

Identifying objects whose names begin with the sound associated with the letter j

## Kk

# king

Recognizing the letter Kk; associating a sound with the letter

# What begins with the sound made by the letter K?

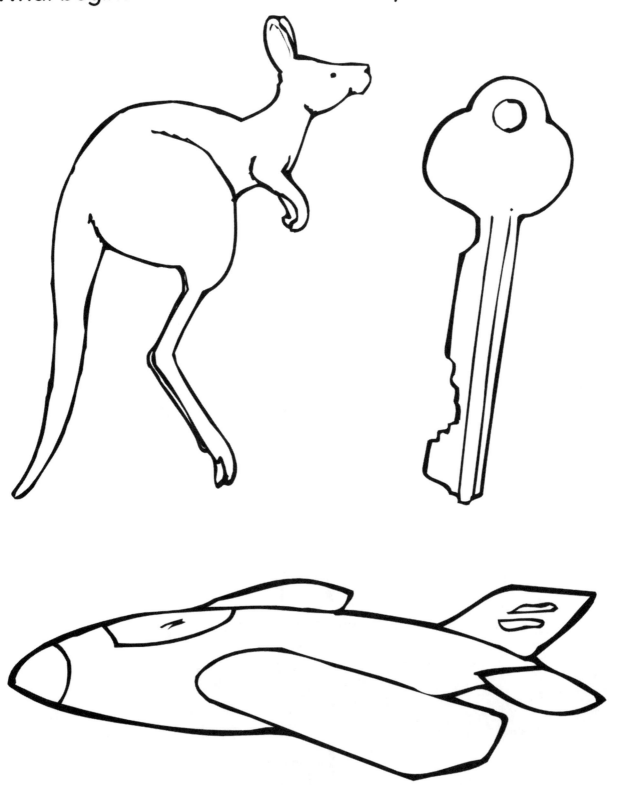

Identifying objects whose names begin with the sound associated with the letter k

lion

Recognizing the letter Ll; associating a sound with the letter

# What begins with the sound made by the letter L?

Alphabet Sounds

**Mm**

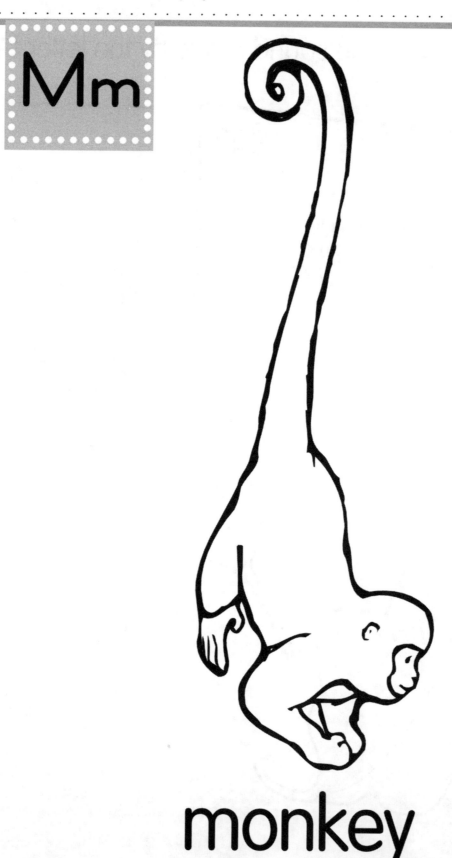

monkey

Recognizing the letter Mm; associating a sound with the letter

# What begins with the sound made by the letter M?

Identifying objects whose names begin with the sound associated with the letter m

# Nn

# nest

Recognizing the letter Nn; associating a sound with the letter

# What begins with the sound made by the letter N?

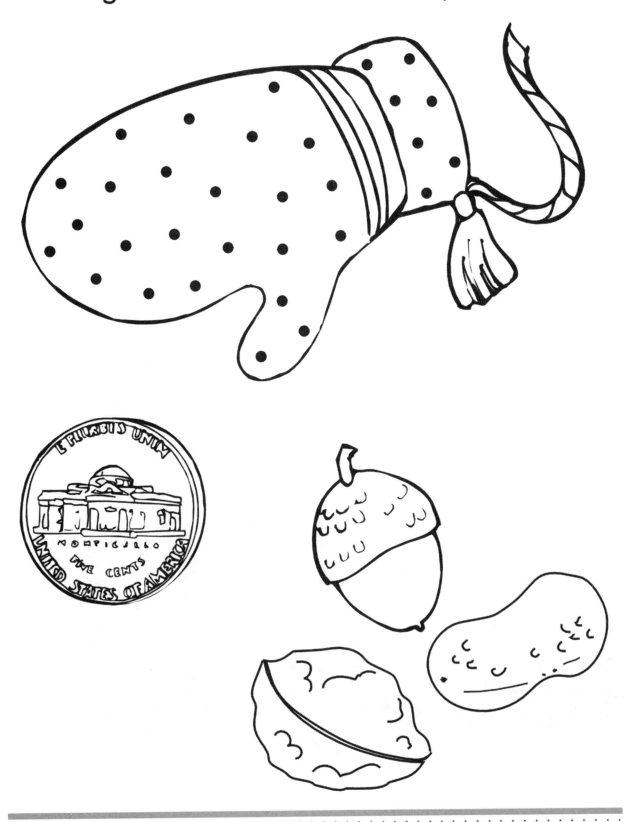

Alphabet Sounds

## Match.

Matching letters with objects whose names begin with sounds associated with them

Match.

H        I

I        k

J        h

K        m

L        i

M        n

N        j

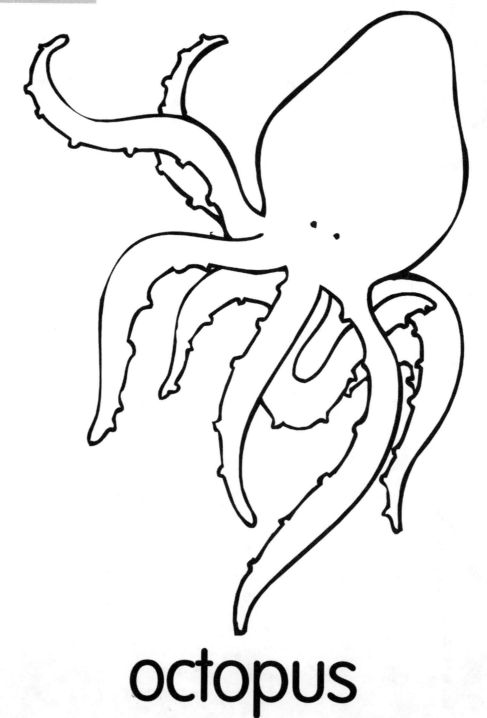

# octopus

Recognizing the letter Oo; associating the short o sound with the letter

# What begins with the sound made by the letter O?

Identifying objects whose names begin with the sound of short o

# P p

**panda**

---

Recognizing the letter Pp; associating a sound with the letter

# What begins with the sound made by the letter P?

Alphabet Sounds

Note: Point to the letter and ask your child to name it. Tell the name if it is unknown to your child. Next ask for the name of the picture and the sound heard at the begining of the word.

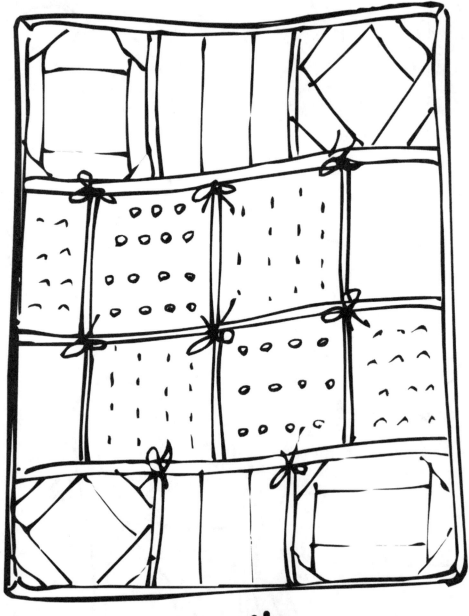

quilt

Recognizing the letter Qq; associating a sound with the letter

# What begins with the sound made by the letter Q?

Alphabet Sounds

# Rr

robot

Recognizing the letter Rr; associating a sound with the letter

# What begins with the sound made by the letter R?

Alphabet Sounds

**Ss**

# seahorse

Recognizing the letter Ss; associating a sound with the letter

# What begins with the sound made by the letter S?

Alphabet Sounds

Identifying objects whose names begin with a sound associated with the letter s

169

## Tt

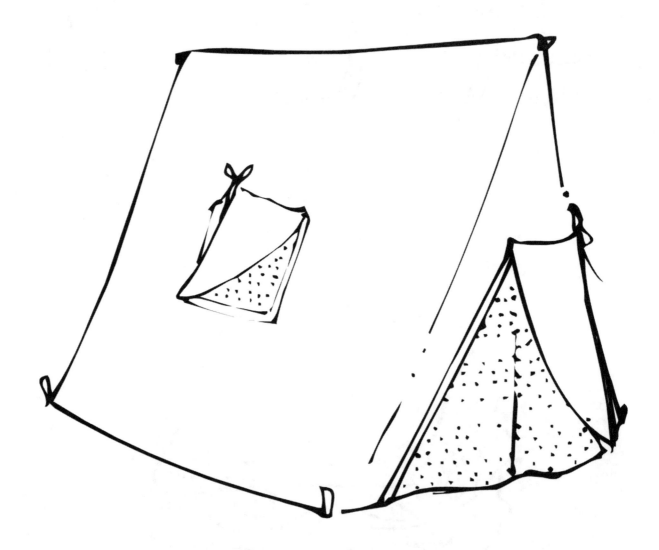

# tent

Recognizing the letter Tt; associating a sound with the letter

Note: Your child may need help in naming the pictures on this page - turtle, telephone, duck.

# What begins with the sound made by the letter T?

Identifying objects whose names begin with the sound associated with the letter t

# Match.

o

p

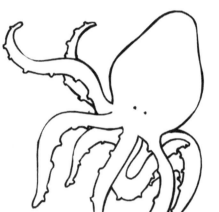

q

r

s

t

Matching letters with objects whose names begin with sounds associated with them

Match.

O

P

Q

R

S

T

p

r

o

s

t

q

Matching capital and lowercase letters

# Uu

# umbrella

Recognizing the letter Uu; associating the short u sound with the letter

# What begins with the sound made by the letter U?

Identifying objects whose names begin with the sound of short u

Alphabet Sounds

# valentine

Recognizing the letter Vv; associating a sound with the letter

# What begins with the sound made by the letter V?

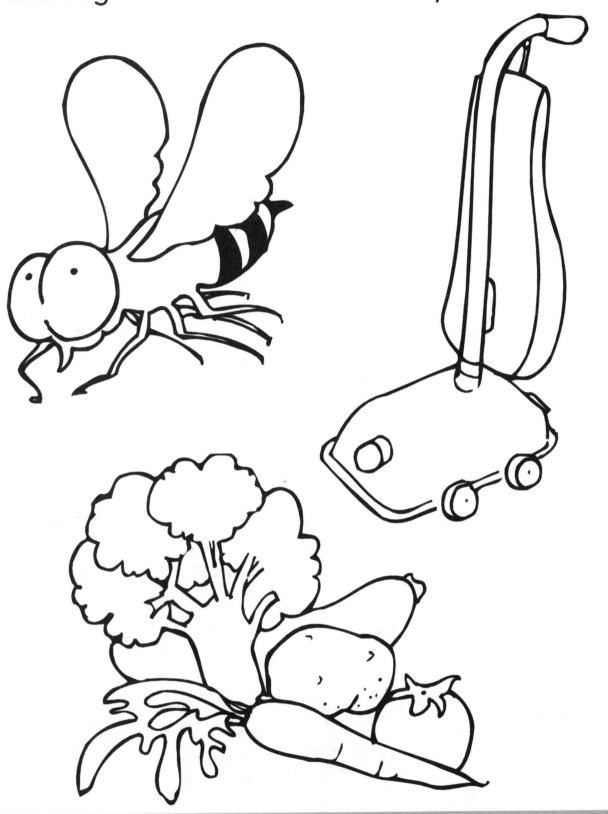

Identifying objects whose names begin with the sound associated with the letter v

Note: Point to the letter and ask your child to name it. Tell the name if it is unknown to your child. Next ask for the name of the picture and the sound heard at the begining of the word.

# wagon

178          Recognizing the letter Ww; associating a sound with the letter

# What begins with the sound made by the letter W?

Identifying objects whose names begin with the sound associated with the letter w          **179**

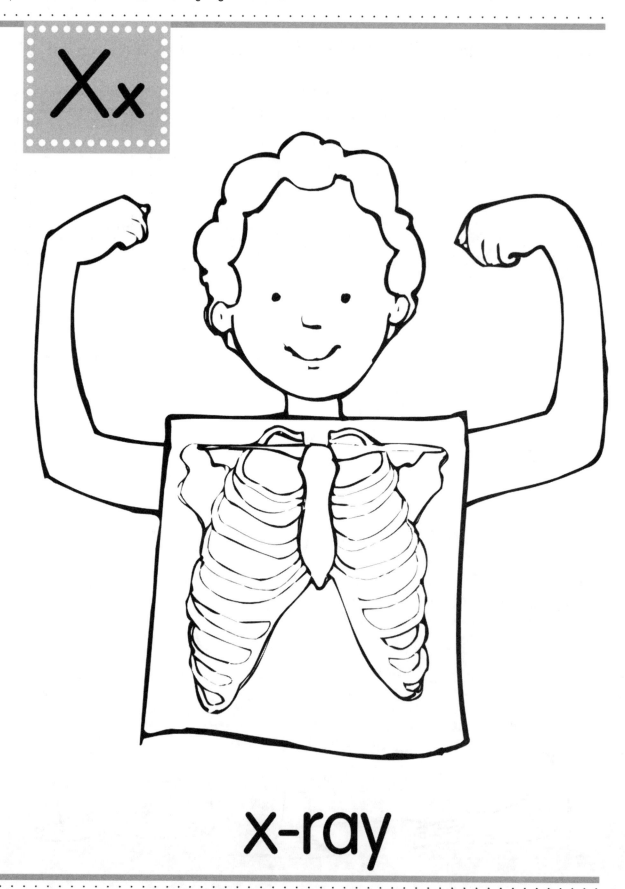

# x-ray

Recognizing the letter Xx; associating a sound with the letter

# Color things that **end** with the sound made by the letter X.

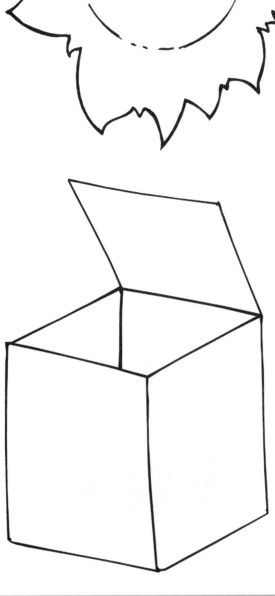

Alphabet Sounds

Note: Point to the letter and ask your child to name it. Tell the name if it is unknown to your child. Next ask for the name of the picture and the sound heard at the begining of the word.

yard

Recognizing the letter Yy; associating a sound with the letter

# What begins with the sound made by the letter Y?

*Identifying objects whose names begin with the sound associated with the letter y*

# Zz

# zebra

Recognizing the letter Zz; associating a sound with the letter

# What begins with the sound of the letter Z?

Alphabet Sounds

Matching letters with objects whose names begin with sounds associated with them

Note: Vowels have two sounds. Pages 61 - 64 contain the long vowel sounds.

Aa

angel

Ee

eagle

Identifying long vowel sounds of a and e

Note: Point to the letter and ask your child to name it. Tell the name if it is unknown to your child. Next ask for the name of the picture and the sound heard at the begining of the word.

I i

ice cream

O o

overalls

U u

unicorn

Identifying long vowel sounds of i, o, and u

Note: Your child may need help in naming the pictures on this page - acorn, pumpkin, king, eel, ivy, ball, square, oval, wagon, unicorn.

# Color the picture that begins with the letter sound.

Identifying objects whose names begin with long vowel sounds

Match each picture to the letter that its name begins with.

Matching vowels with objects whose names begin with their long sounds

# Answer Key

Please take time to go over the work your child has completed. Ask your child to explain what he/she has done. Praise both success and effort. If mistakes have been made, explain what the answer should have been and how to find it. Let your child know that mistakes are a part of learning. The time you spend with your child helps let him/her know you feel learning is important.

**page 129**

**page 131**

**page 133**

**page 135**

**page 137**

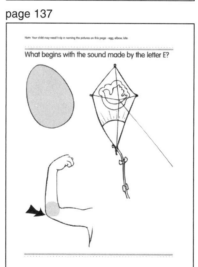

**page 139**

**page 141**

**page 142**

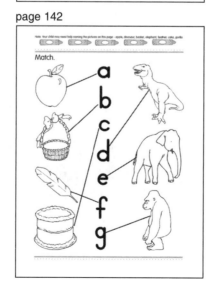

**page 143**

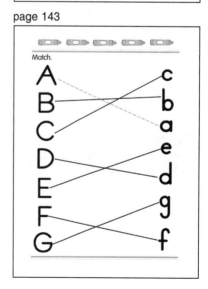

page 145

Note: Your child may need help in naming the pictures on this page - hot dog, hen, astronaut.

What begins with the sound made by the letter H?

page 147

Note: Your child may need help in naming the pictures on this page - igloo, in, ant.

What begins with the sound made by the letter I?

page 149

Note: Your child may need help in naming the pictures on this page - jacket, jeep, kite.

What begins with the sound made by the letter J?

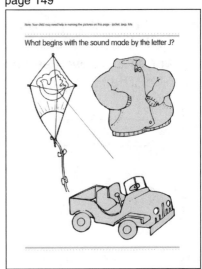

page 151

Note: Your child may need help in naming the pictures on this page - kangaroo, key, jet.

What begins with the sound made by the letter K?

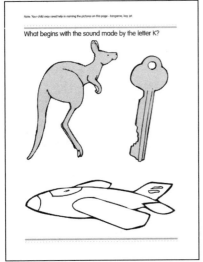

page 153

Note: Your child may need help in naming the pictures on this page - letter, leaf, feather.

What begins with the sound made by the letter L?

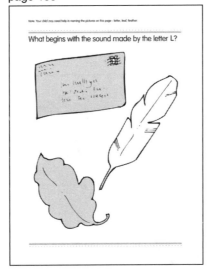

page 155

Note: Your child may need help in naming the pictures on this page - mitten, mouse, net.

What begins with the sound made by the letter M?

page 157

Note: Your child may need help in naming the pictures on this page - nuts, nickel, mitten.

What begins with the sound made by the letter N?

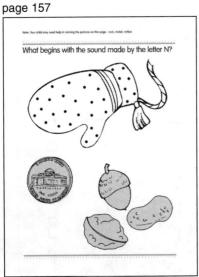

page 158

Note: Your child may need help in naming the pictures on this page - jacket, leaf, key, igloo, hen, mitten, nest.

Match.

page 159

Match.

Answers

**page 161**

Note: Your child may need help in naming the pictures on this page - ostrich, olive, apple.

What begins with the sound made by the letter O?

**page 163**

Note: Your child may need help in naming the pictures on this page - pumpkin, pig, goat.

What begins with the sound made by the letter P?

**page 165**

Note: Your child may need help in naming the pictures on this page - queen, quail, pie.

What begins with the sound made by the letter Q?

**page 167**

Note: Your child may need help in naming the pictures on this page - rabbit, ring, walrus.

What begins with the sound made by the letter R?

**page 169**

Note: Your child may need help in naming the pictures on this page - sandwich, scissors, cow.

What begins with the sound made by the letter S?

**page 171**

Note: Your child may need help in naming the pictures on this page - turtle, telephone, duck.

What begins with the sound made by the letter T?

**page 172**

Note: Your child may need help in naming the pictures on this page - pig, queen, octopus, turtle, scissors, robot.

Match.

**page 173**

Match.

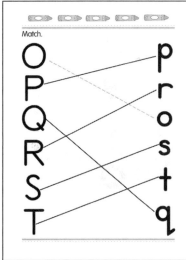

**page 175**

Note: Your child may need help in naming the pictures on this page - umpire, up, web.

What begins with the sound made by the letter U?

Alphabet Sounds

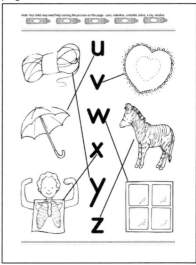

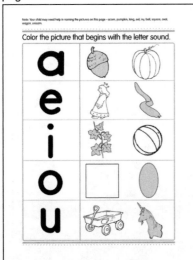

# Color.

**a
green**

a green

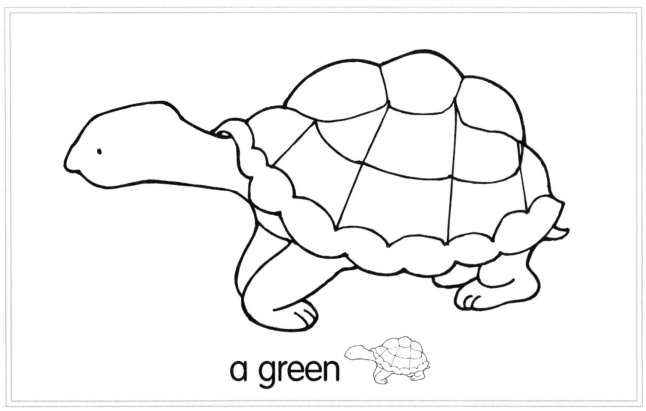

a green

Reading color words; reading sight word a          195

Note: Help your child read the words.

# Color.

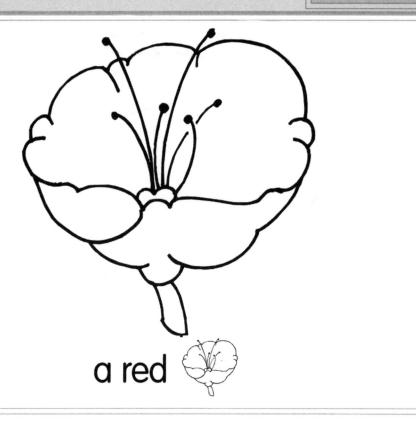

a red

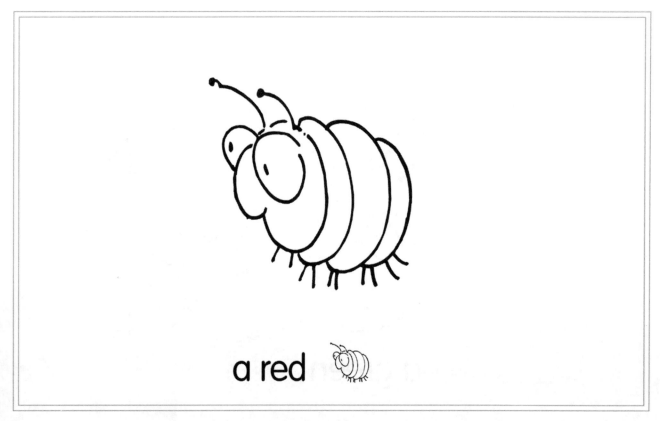

a red

196                    Reading color words

Note: Help your child read the words.

# Color.

is
and

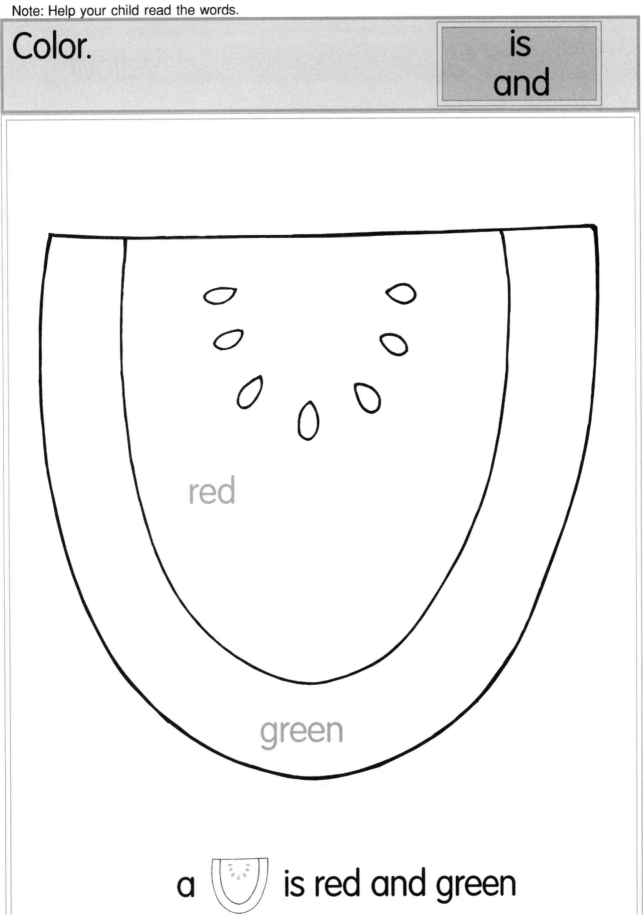

red

green

a 🍉 is red and green

# Color.

yellow

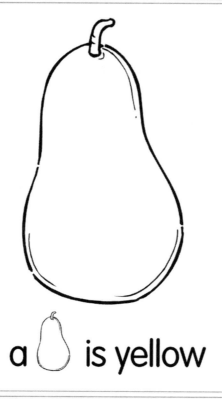

a 🍐 is yellow

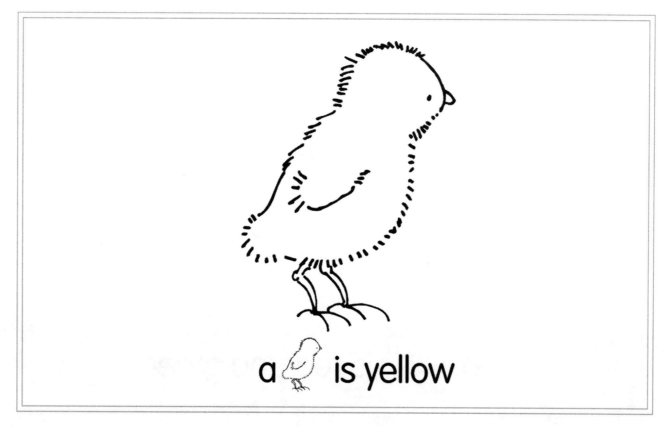

a 🐤 is yellow

Reading color words

Note: Help your child read the words.

# Color.

blue

a blue

a blue

# Color.

See

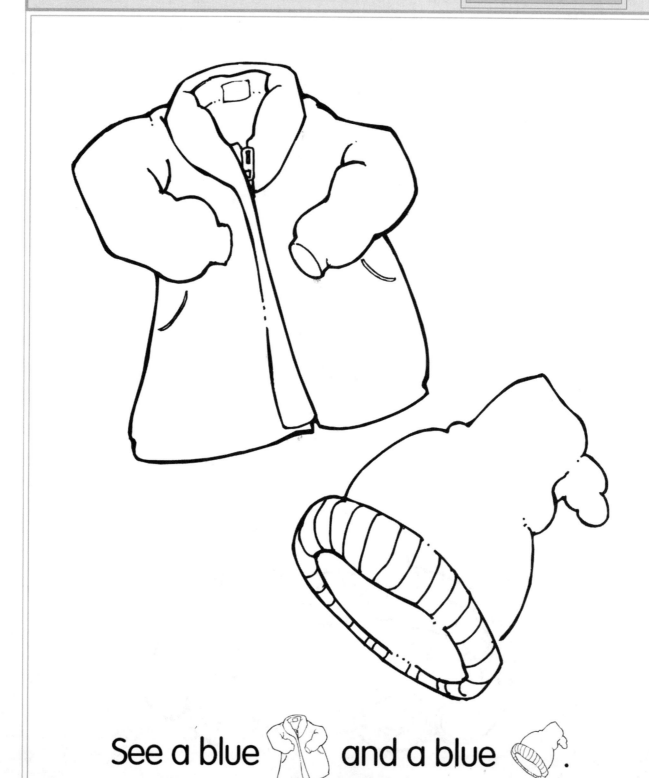

See a blue and a blue .

Reading color words; reading sight word See

Note: Help your child read the words.

# Color.

A
in

A green 🐸 is in blue 〰️ .

Reading color words; reading sight words A, in

# Color.

the
See

yellow

red

blue

green          green

See the 🧍 .

Reading color words; reading sight words see, the

Note: Help your child read the words.

# Color.

one

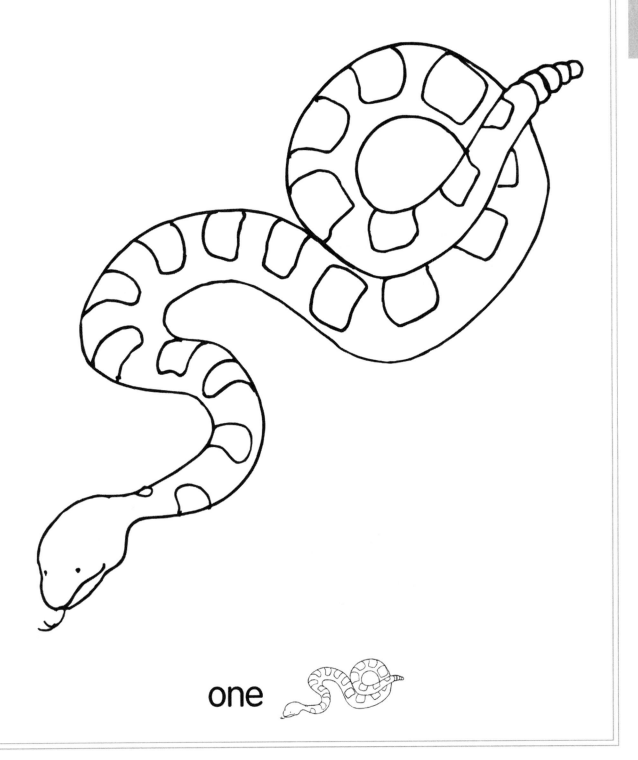

one

# Color.

one
and

one blue 🍵 and one red ⬭

Reading color words and number words

# Color.

two

two

# Color.

three

Reading number words

Note: Help your child read the words.

# Cut and paste.

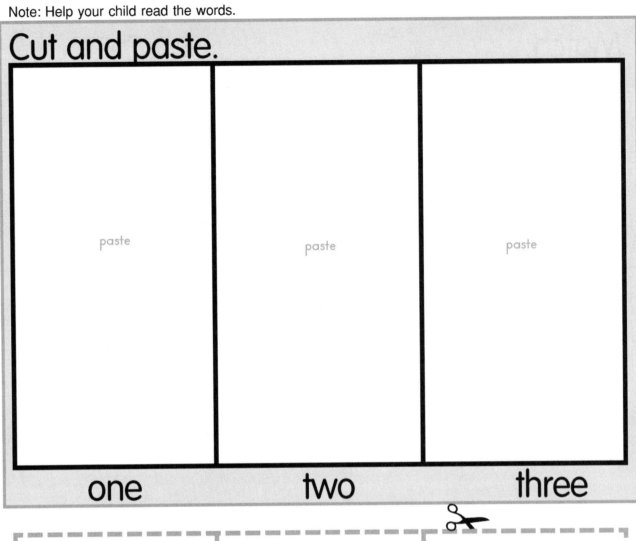

| one | two | three |

Reading number words; counting

## Match:

2         one

3         three

1         two

Matching numerals with number words

Note: Help your child read the words.

# Match.

See two____.

See one____.

See three____.

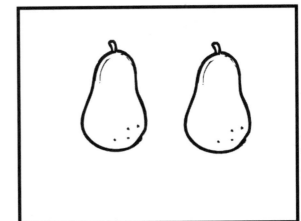

# Color.

brown

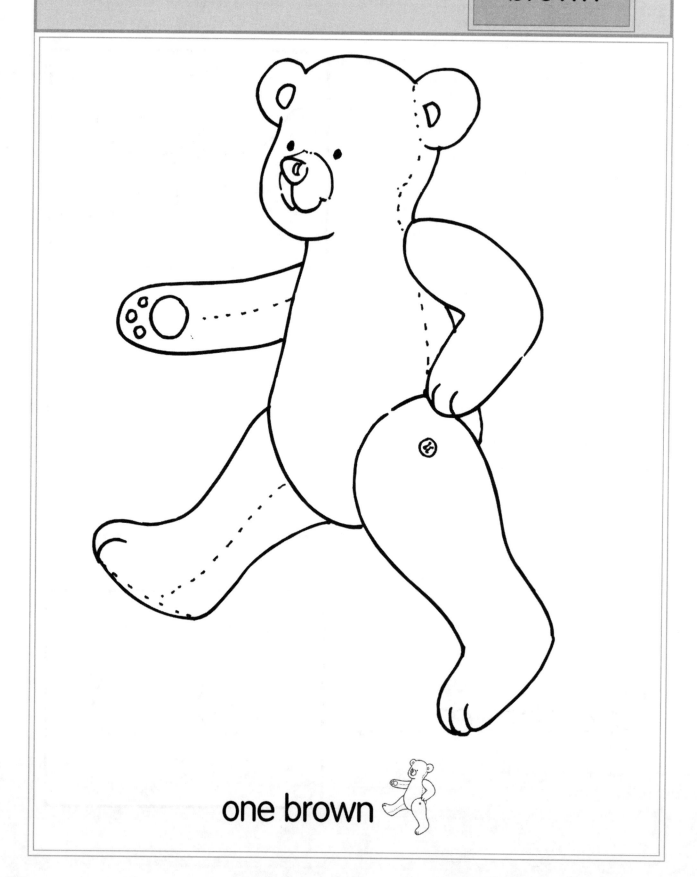

one brown

Reading color words and number words

Note: Help your child read the words.

# Color.

three

a brown

# Draw.

three brown

Reading color words and number words; drawing a specified number of objects

# Color.

orange

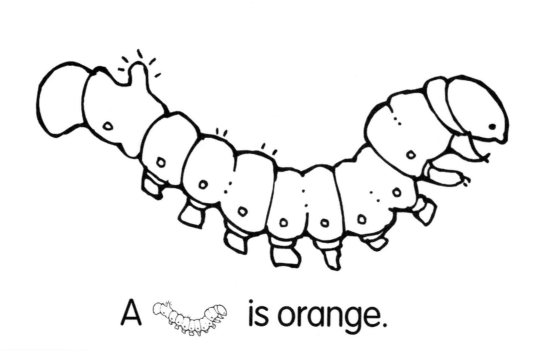

A 🐛 is orange.

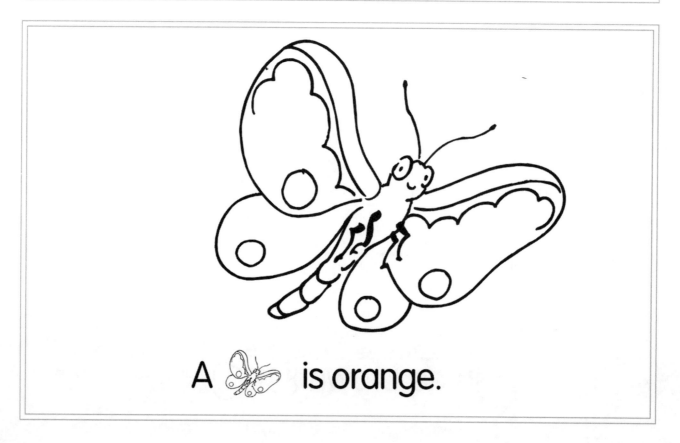

A 🦋 is orange.

Reading color words and sight words

Note: Help your child read the words.

# Color.

The
the
on

The  ⬡ is orange.
Draw 😊 on the ⬡.

# Color.

brown

orange

orange

brown

orange

See the brown [image: cat] .
The [image: scarf] is orange.

Reading color words and sight words

Note: Help your child read the words.

# Draw .

one green

two blue

three red

Note: Your child is to put one letter in each box to spell a word. Explain that tall letters go in tall boxes and short letters go in short boxes.

# Fill in the boxes.

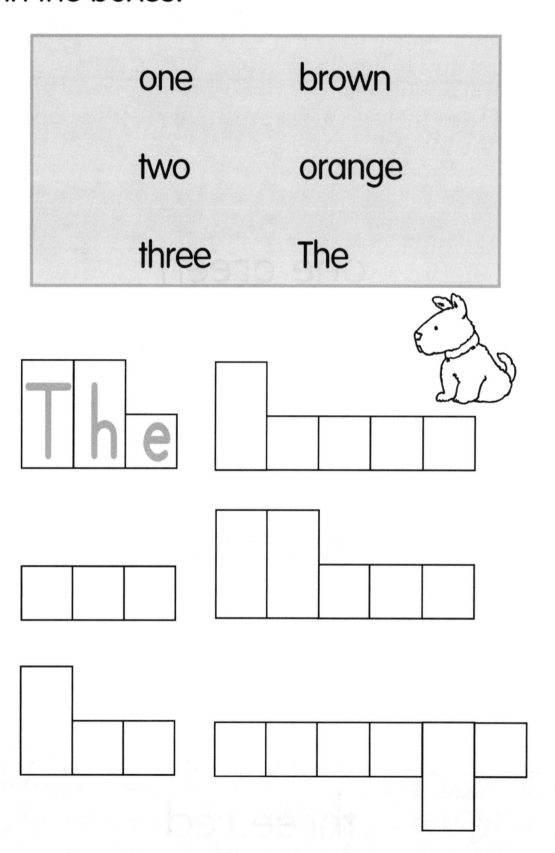

*Associating words with their shapes*

Note: Help your child read the words.

# Color.

bat
black

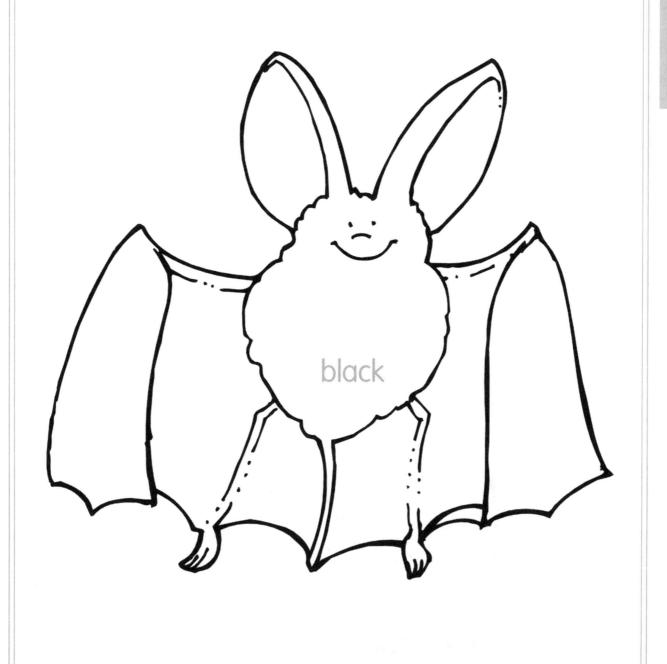

A bat is black.

Reading color words; reading short vowel words: bat, black

## Color.

Make
cat
hat

black

See a black cat.
Make a hat on the cat.

Note: Help your child read the words.

# Color.

big

brown

a big

Reading color words; reading short vowel word big

Note: Help your child read the words.

# Read and color.

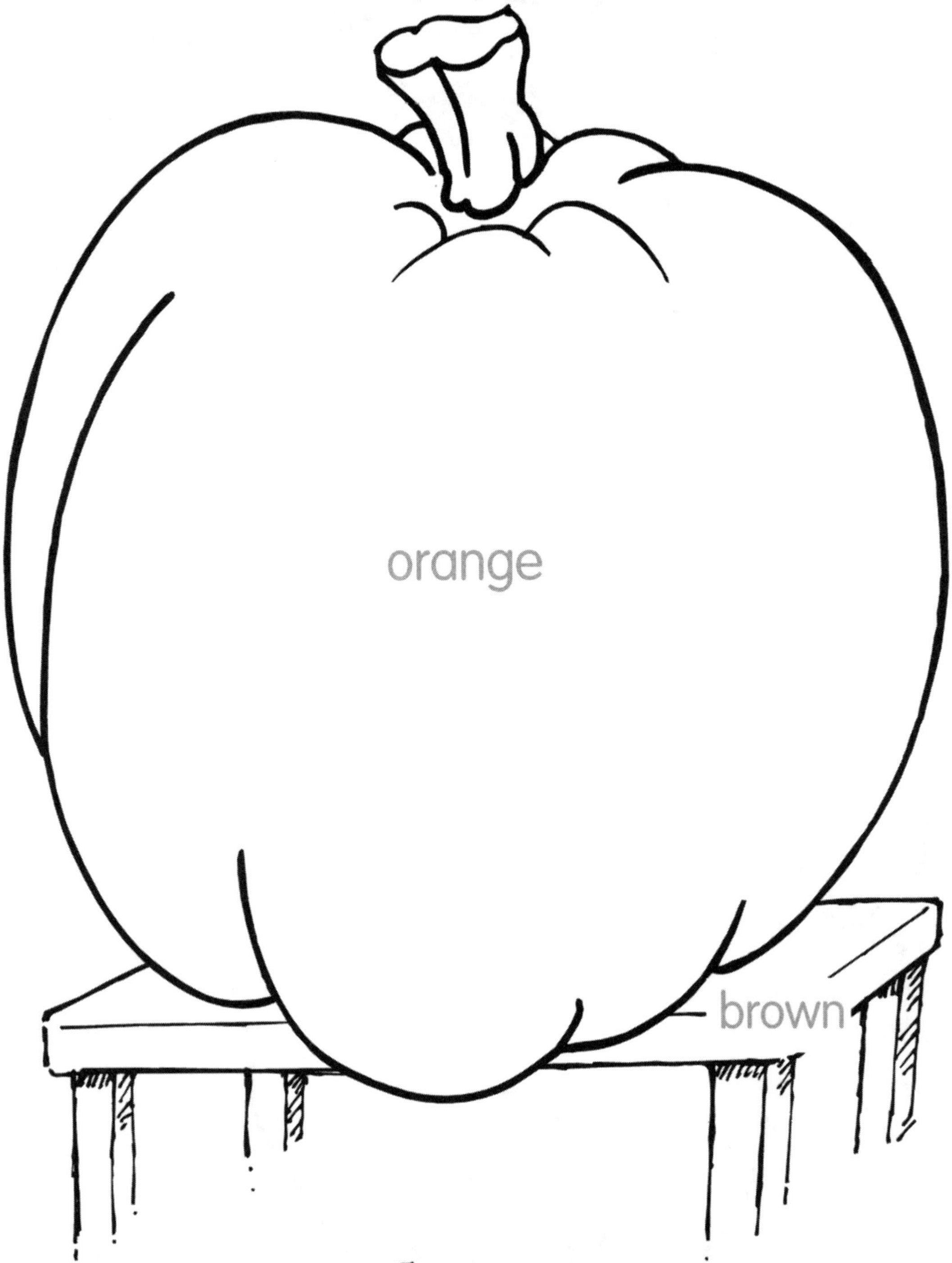

The big  is on a 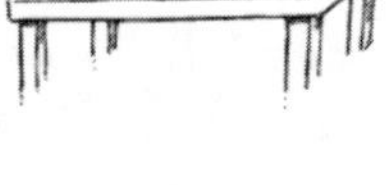 .

Note: Help your child read the words.

# Read and color.

littile

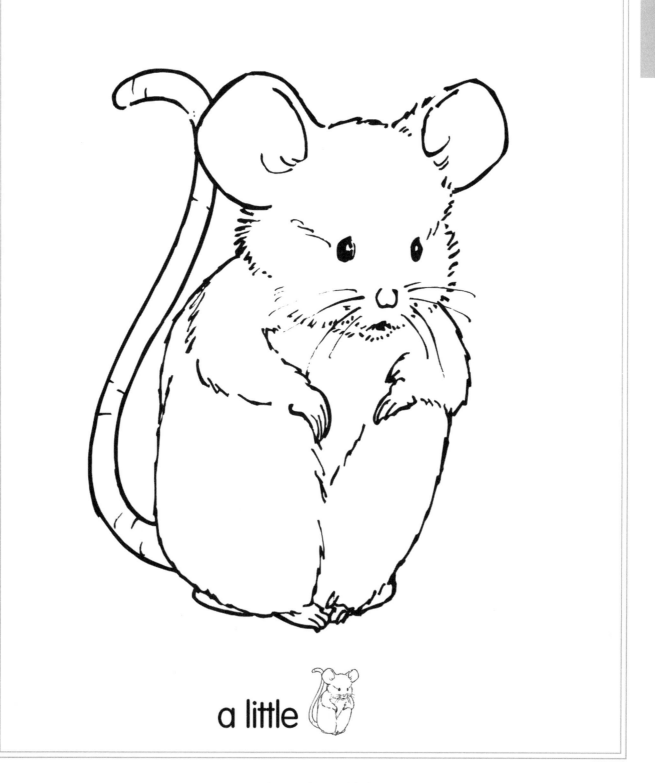

a little

Note: Help your child read the words.

# Draw on the  .

one big

two big

Reading number words and a short vowel word; following directions

Note: Help your child read the words.

# Cut and paste.

| big | little |
|---|---|
| paste | paste |
| paste | paste |

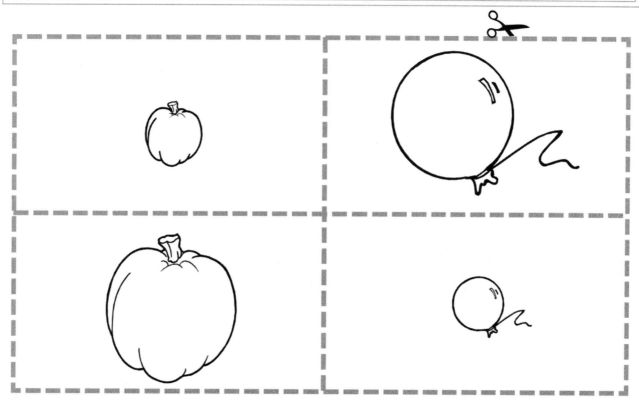

Reading short vowel words; classifying objects and pictures

# Match.

big

little

Matching short vowel words with objects and pictures

# Color.

purple

a purple and purple

## Read and color.

box

one big cat on a 🛏
two little 🐭 in a box

Reading short vowel word box; reading sight words; reading number words

Note: Your child is to cut out the chicks and paste them in the nest.

# Cut and paste

Put

Put three little  on the big  .

Reading sight word put; reading number words, sight words, and short vowel words; following directions    **227**

# Match.

three

one

two

Matching number words with sets of objects

Note: Your child is to put one letter in each box to spell a word. Explain that tall letters go in tall boxes and short letters go in short boxes.

# Fill in the boxes.

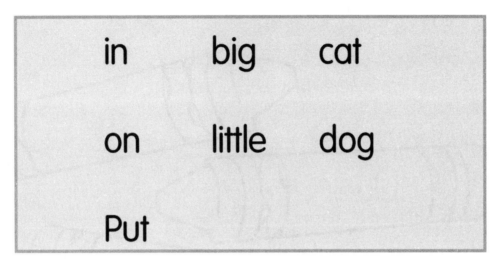

in   big   cat

on   little   dog

Put

P u t

# Color.

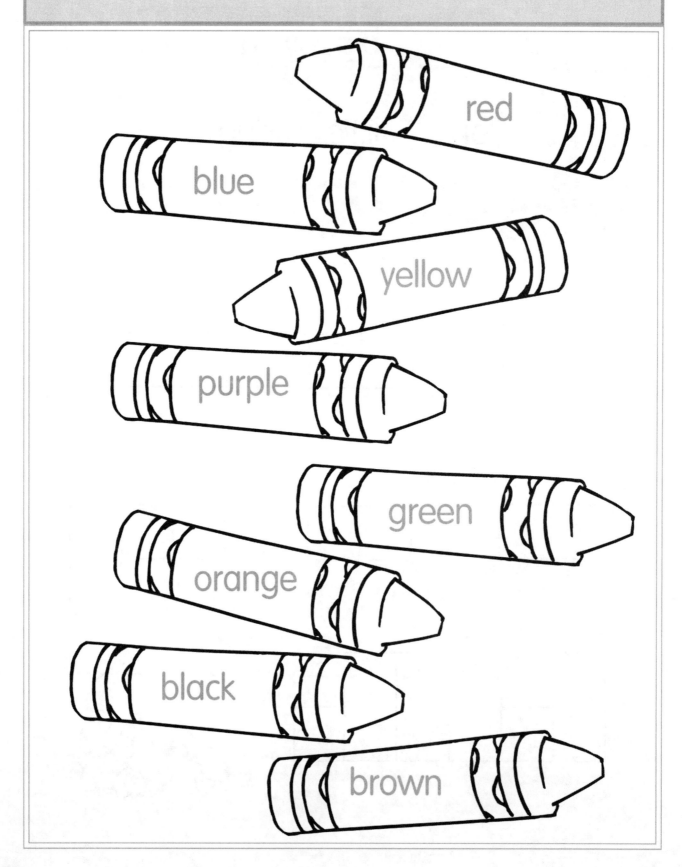

Reading color words

Note: Help your child read the words.

## Cut and paste.

The hat is red.
Put it on the  .

The  is blue.
Put it on the  .

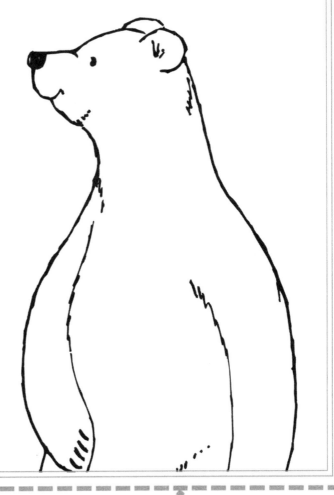

red

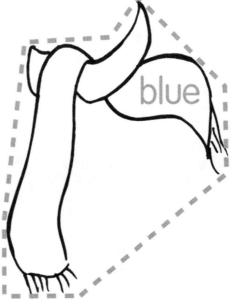

blue

*Following directions that contain color words, sight words, and short vowel words*

# Color.

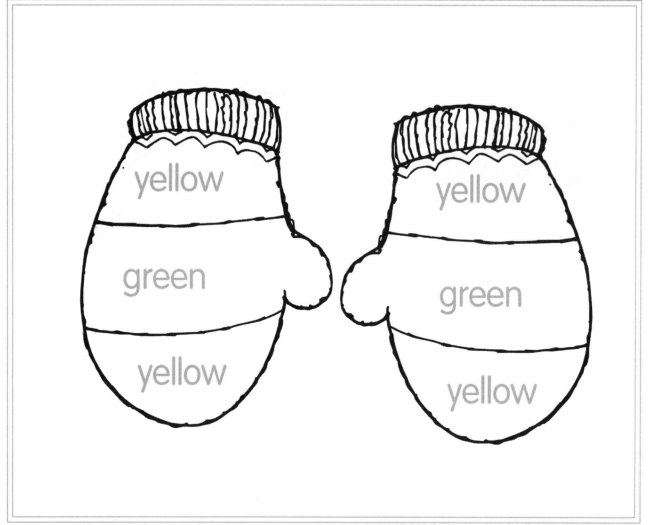

Reading color words

Note: Help your child read the words.

# Read and color.

run
can
Can

purple

blue

yellow

The 🏃 can run.
Can the dog run?

# Read and color.

brown

black

The big dog can run.
Can the little dog run?
Put X on the big dog.

Note: Help your child read the words.

# Read and color.

It
jump
frog

green

See the frog.
It is big.
It can jump.

Reading color words; reading short vowel words it, jump, frog

# Read and color.

fox

brown

See the little fox.
The fox can run.
Can it jump?

Reading a color word; reading the short vowel word fox

Note: Help your child read the words.

# Read and color.

blue

yellow

red

black

A 🧍☂ is in the ☔️.
Put X on the ☂.

Reading color words; following directions

Note: Help your child read the words.

# Read and color.

sun
fun

It is fun to run in the sun.

Reading short vowel words sun, fun

Note: Help your child read the words.

# Read and color.

bug
rug

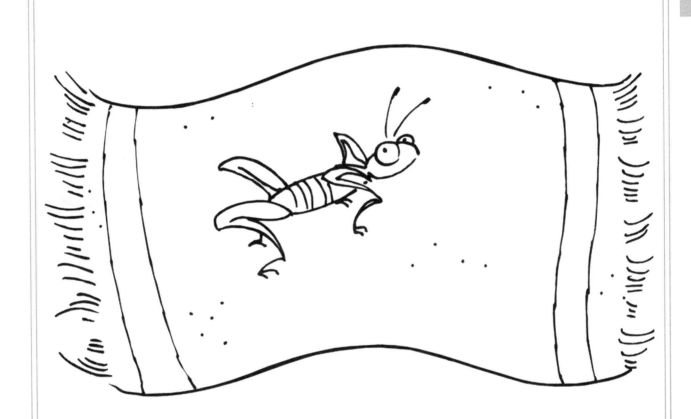

See the black bug.
It is on a red rug.
Can it jump?

Reading color words; reading short vowel words bug, rug

Note: Your child is to put one letter in each box to spell a word. Explain that tall letters go in tall boxes and short letters go in short boxes.

# Fill in the blanks.

Put    can    rug    hat

jump    It    bug    it

Associating words with their shapes

Note: Help your child read the words.

# Cut and paste.

| | |
|---|---|
| paste | paste |
| **cat** | **frog** |
| paste | paste |
| **dog** | **bug** |

Matching pictures of objects with the short vowel words that name them

# Draw.

| | |
|---|---|
| a big cat | a little bug |

Following directions that contain sight words and short vowel words

Note: Your child is to match the words. Ask her/him to read the words to you.

# Match.

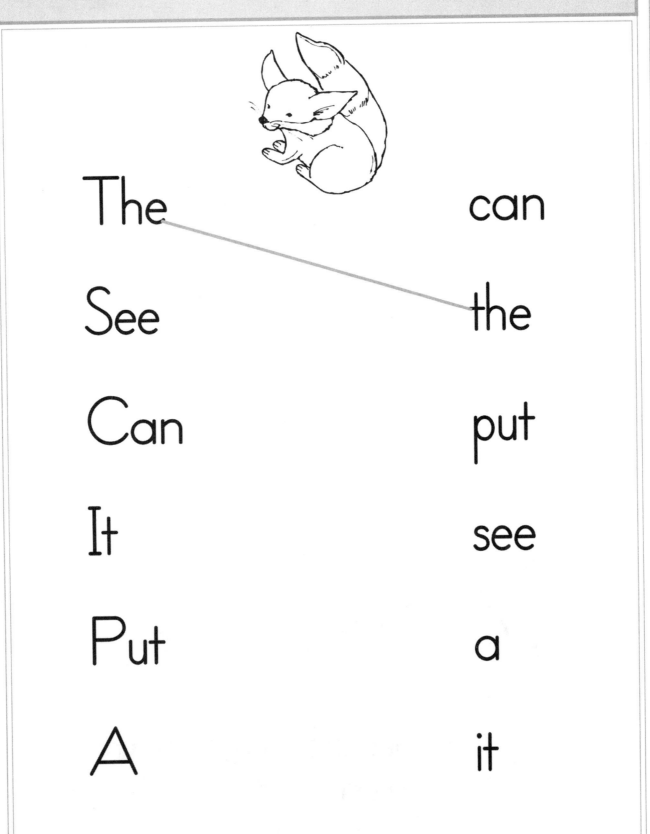

The                    can

See                    the

Can                    put

It                     see

Put                    a

A                      it

Matching capitalized words and lowercase words          **243**

# Read and color.

He

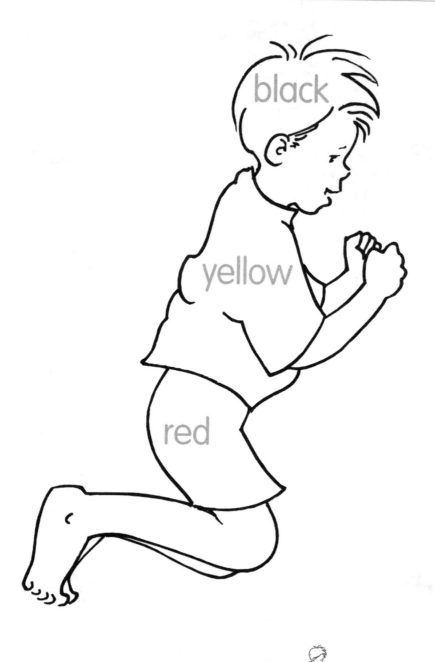

black

yellow

red

See the .
He can run.
He can jump.

Reading color words, short vowel words, and the sight word he

Note: Help your child read the words.

# Cut and paste.

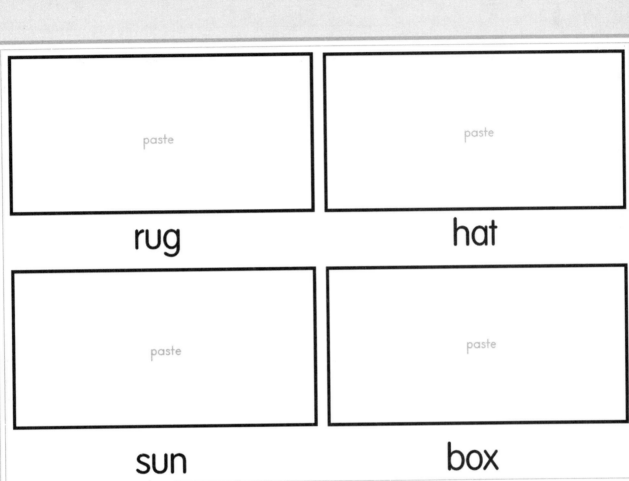

rug

hat

sun

box

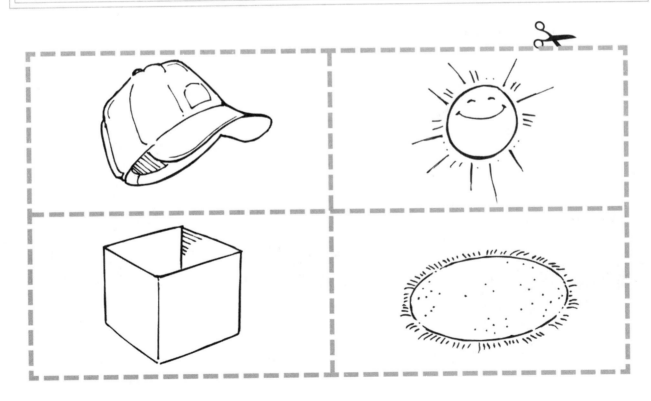

Matching pictures of objects with the short vowel words that name them

# Draw.

| | |
|---|---|
| a yellow sun | a black hat |

Following directions that contain color words, sight words, and short vowel words

# Read and draw.

Make

Draw a little frog.
Put it in the  .
Make the frog green.

Following directions that contain color words, sight words, and short vowel words

# Word Cards

Pages 249, 251, and 253 provide word cards for 30 of the words practiced in this book.

Cut the cards apart. Store them in a sturdy envelope, small box, or zipper-lock bag.

Two suggestions for using the word cards are given below.

## Reading Practice

1. Select a few cards at a time to review with your child. Choose words your child has already been introduced to on the activity pages.

2. Show one card at a time. Ask your child to read the word. If he/she has difficulty, say the word yourself. Go through the words no more than three to five times during one practice time.

3. Review the same words and add one or two new words at the next practice session. Continue until all the words have been learned.

## Matching

1. Give your child the following word cards:

| a | the | see | put | can |

2. Lay out these cards:

| A | The | See | Put | Can |

3. Ask him/her to match your cards.

## Make More Word Cards

Not all words introduced in this book are included in the word cards on pages 249, 251, and 253. You may want to make additional word cards for these words:

| bat | sun | frog | cat | fun | bug |
| hat | boy | rug | Make | fox | He |

Reading color words, number words, sight words, and short vowel words

| | |
|---|---|
| red | blue |
| green | yellow |
| black | brown |
| orange | purple |
| big | little |

Reading color words, number words, sight words, and short vowel words

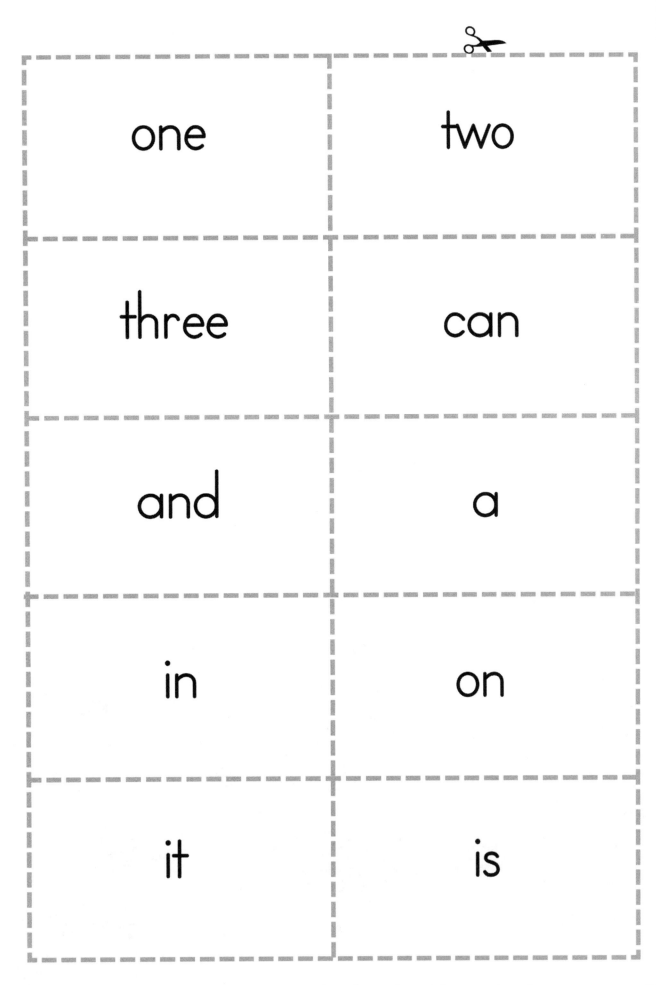

| one | two |
| three | can |
| and | a |
| in | on |
| it | is |

jump

run

see

the

Put

Can

A

It

The

See

# Answer Key

Please take time to go over the work your child has completed. Ask your child to explain what he/she has done. Praise both success and effort. If mistakes have been made, explain what the answer should have been and how to find it. Let your child know that mistakes are a part of learning. The time you spend with your child helps let him/her know you feel learning is important.

page 201

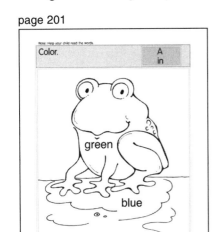

page 204

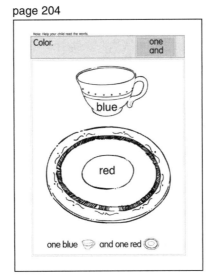

page 207

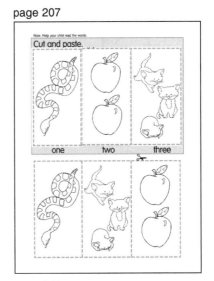

page 208

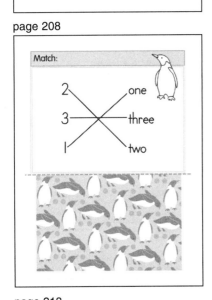

page 209

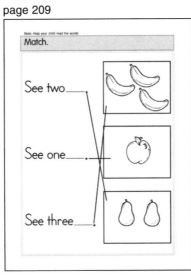

page 211

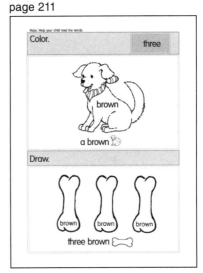

page 213

page 215

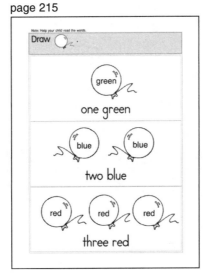

page 216

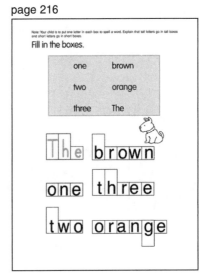

**page 218**

Note: Help your child read the words.
Color.

Make
cat
hat

See a black cat.
Make a hat on the cat.

**page 222**

Note: Help your child read the words.
Draw on the 🐶

one big 🎩
two big ⚫

**page 223**

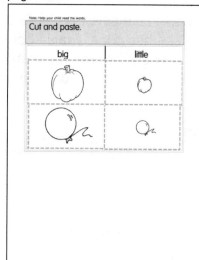

Note: Help your child read the words.
Cut and paste.

| big | little |
|-----|--------|
|  |  |
|  |  |

**page 224**

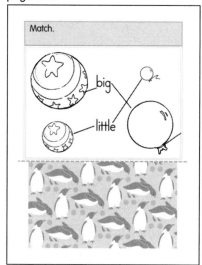

Match.

big

little

**page 227**

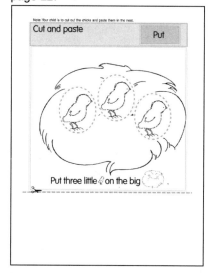

Note: Your child is to cut out the chicks and paste them in the nest.
Cut and paste

Put

Put three little 🐤 on the big 🪹

**page 228**

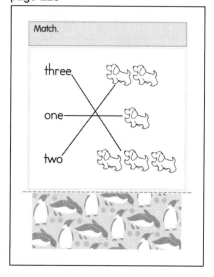

Match.

three

one

two

**page 229**

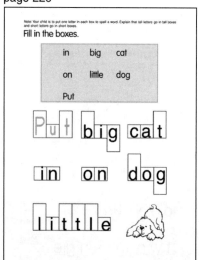

Note: Your child is to put one letter in each box to spell a word. Explain that tall letters go in tall boxes and short letters go in short boxes.
Fill in the boxes.

| in | big | cat |
|----|-----|-----|
| on | little | dog |
| Put |  |  |

Put big cat

in on dog

little

**page 231**

Note: Help your child read the words.
Cut and paste.

The hat is red.
Put it on the 🐻.

The 🧣 is blue.
Put it on the 🐻.

red

blue

**page 234**

Note: Help your child read the words.
Read and color.

brown

black

The big dog can run.
Can the little dog run?
Put X on the big dog.

page 237

page 239

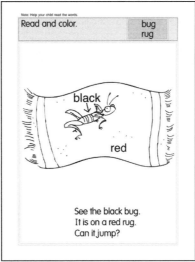

page 240

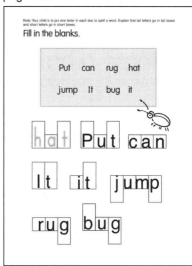

page 241

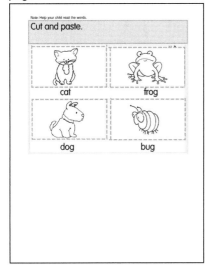

page 242

page 243

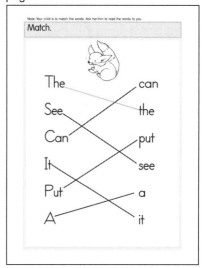

page 245

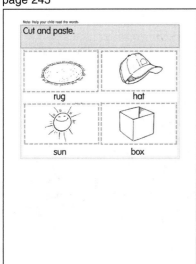

page 246

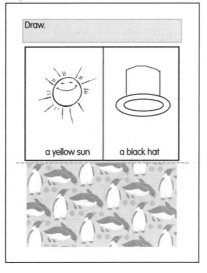

page 247

Answers

# Is there a hat for each clown?     yes     no

Understanding one-to-one correspondence

Note: Help your child discover that the items in the picture correspond to the numbers being practiced.

## Trace and write.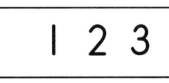

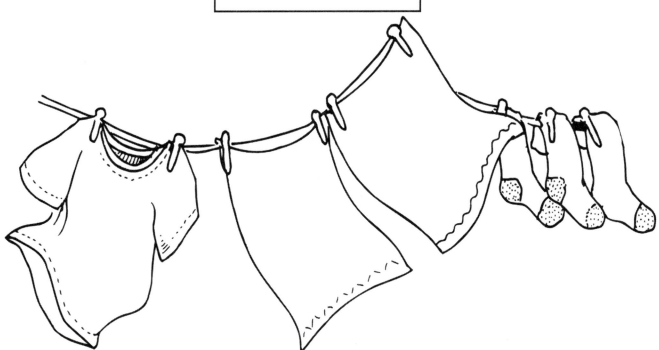

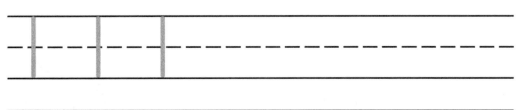

Color the set of 1 green.
Color the set of 2 blue.
Color the set of 3 orange.

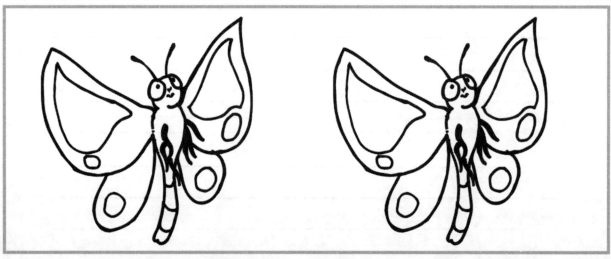

Counting

# Cut out the bees.
# Paste them on the correct hives.

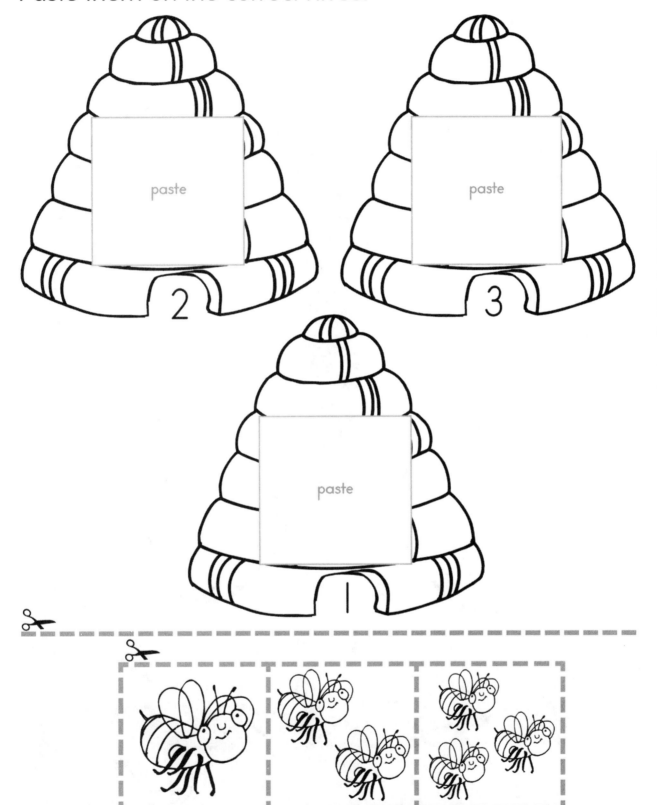

Getting Ready for Math

# Color the picture.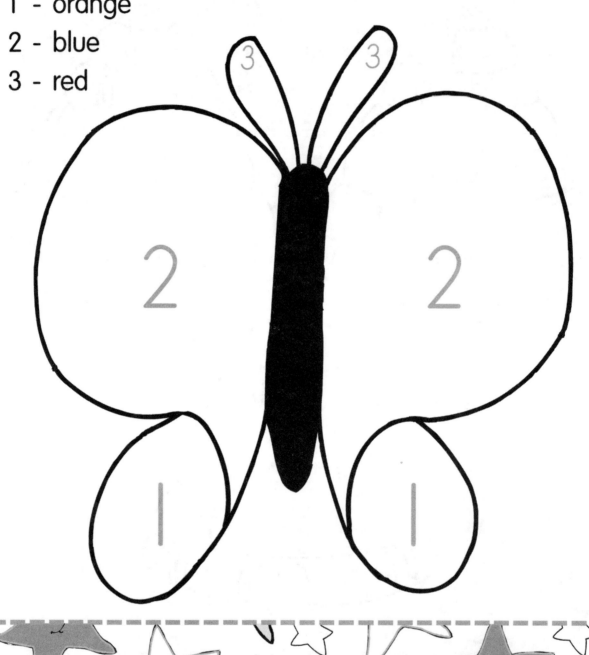

1 - orange

2 - blue

3 - red

Recognizing numerals; following directions

# Connect the dots.

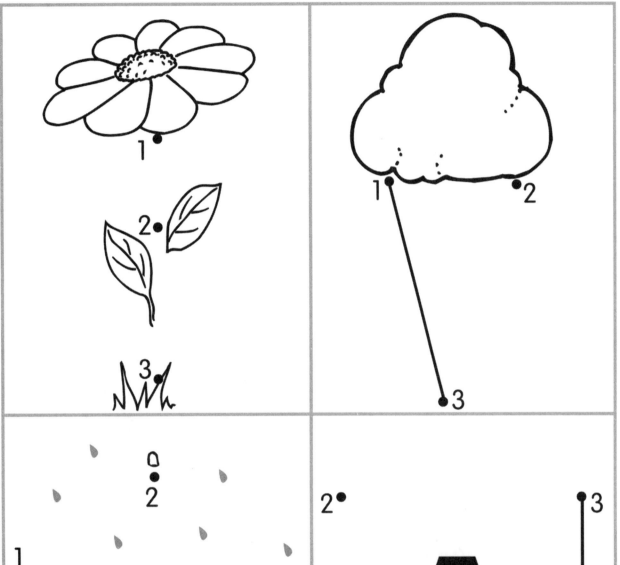

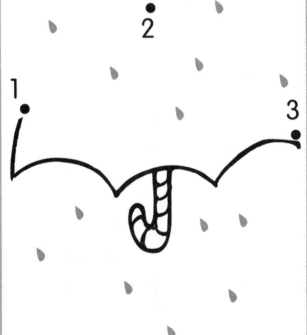

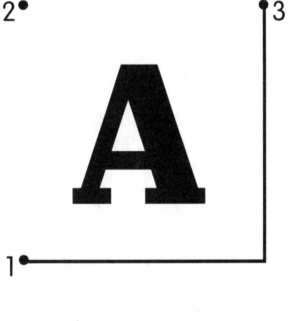

# How many are in each set?

1   2   3

1   2   3

2   3   1

2   3   1

3   2   1

3   2   1

Counting objects and matching with a numeral

## Trace and write.

| 4 | 5 | 6 |

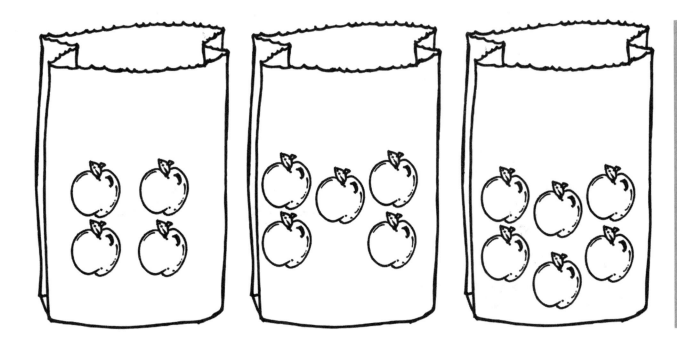

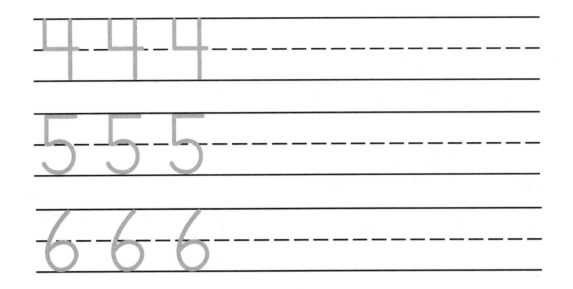

# How many are in each set?

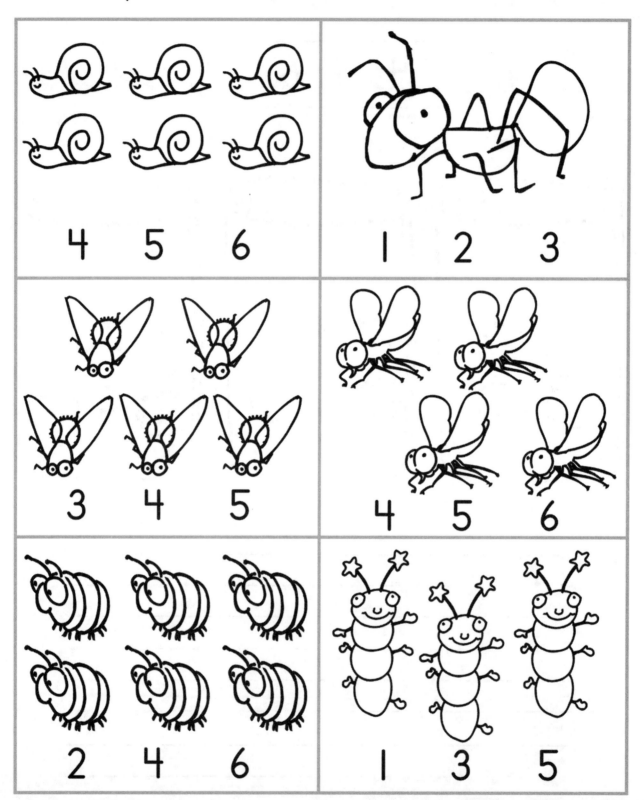

4  5  6

1  2  3

3  4  5

4  5  6

2  4  6

1  3  5

Counting objects and matching with a numeral

# Draw the correct number of dots on the clown hats.

Drawing objects to match a given number

Color the set of 4 green.
Color the set of 5 blue.
Color the set of 6 brown.

Counting

# Cut out the apples.
# Paste them on the correct trees.

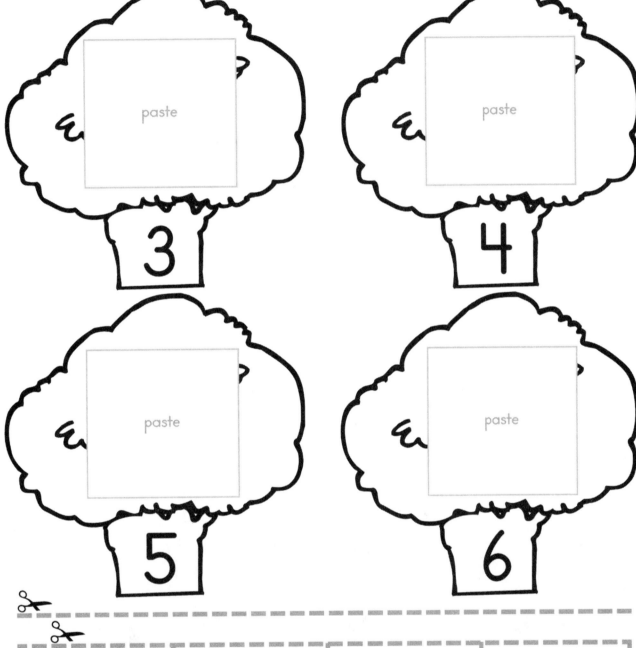

Counting objects and matching with a numeral

Connect the dots.

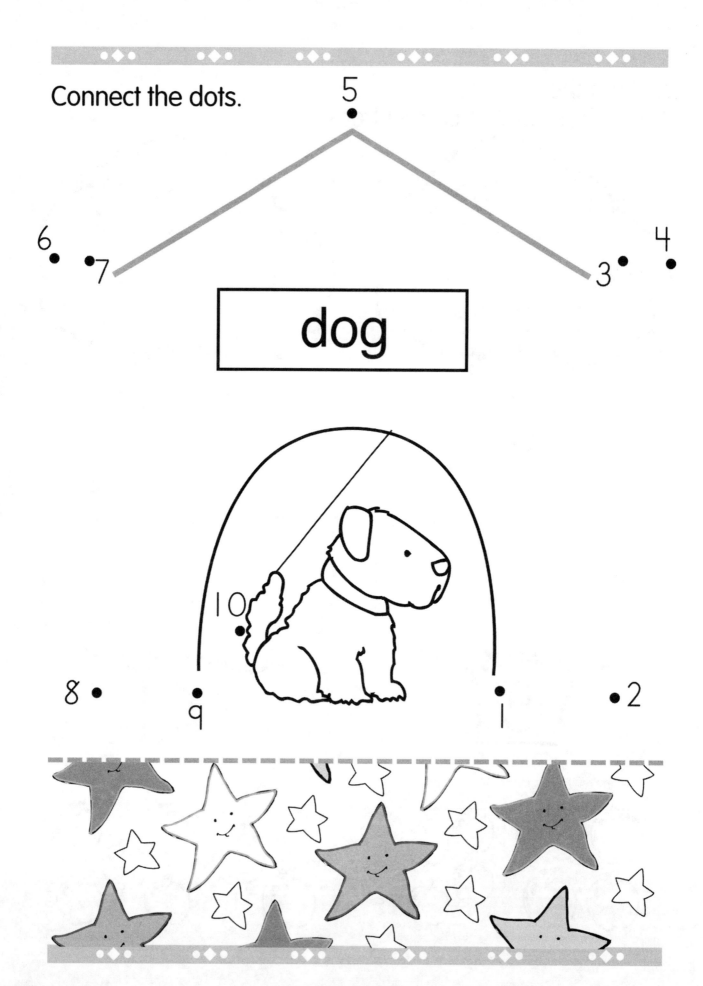

dog

Understanding number order

Color the picture.

1 - green
2 - yellow
3 - orange

white

white

black

black

Recognizing numerals; following directions

# How many are in each set?

4   5   6

1   2   3

3   4   5

6   2   4

1   3   5

5   2   6

Counting objects and matching with a numeral

# Cut out the numbers.
# Paste them in order.

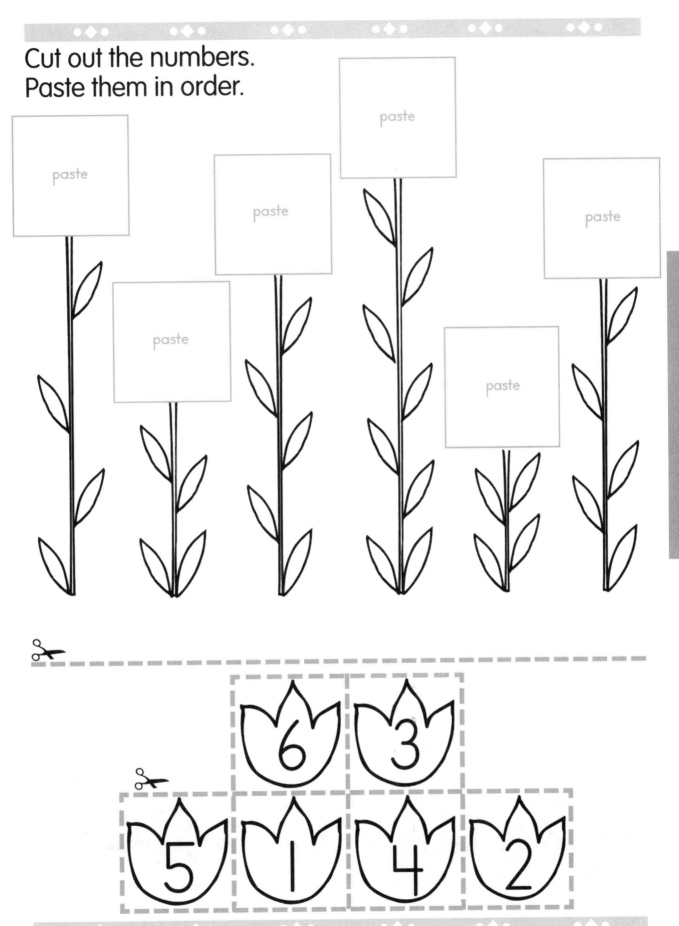

# Fill in the missing numbers.

| 1 2 3 4 5 6 |

2 __3__

__ 3

4 __

__ 6

1 __

__ 4

5 __

__ 2

Understanding number order

# Draw the correct number of petals on the flowers.

# Trace and write.

7

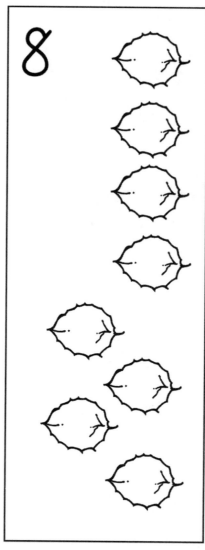

8

9

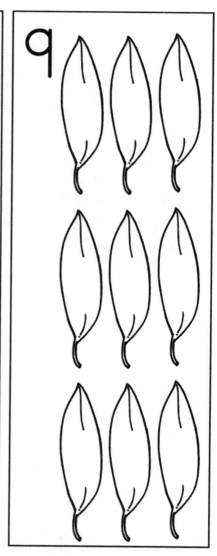

7 7 7 - - - - - - - - - - - - - - - - -

8 8 8 - - - - - - - - - - - - - - - - -

9 9 9 - - - - - - - - - - - - - - - - -

Tracing and writing numerals; counting

Color the set of 6 purple.

Color the set of 7 orange.

Color the set of 8 yellow.

Color the set of 9 red.

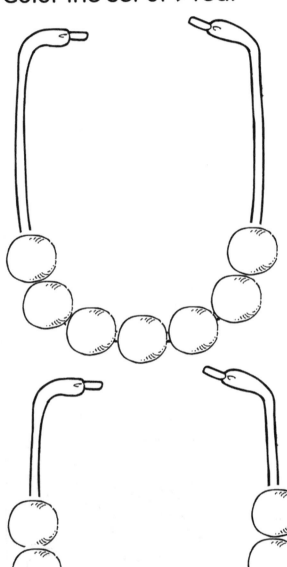

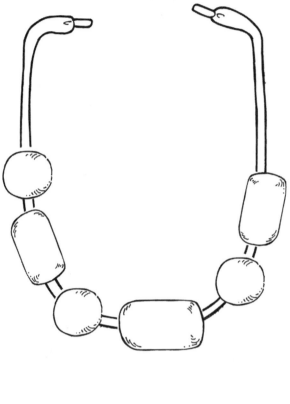

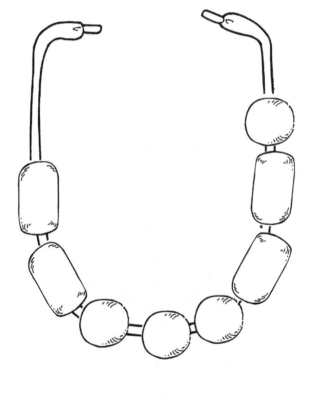

Understanding quantities represented by numbers

# How many are in each set?

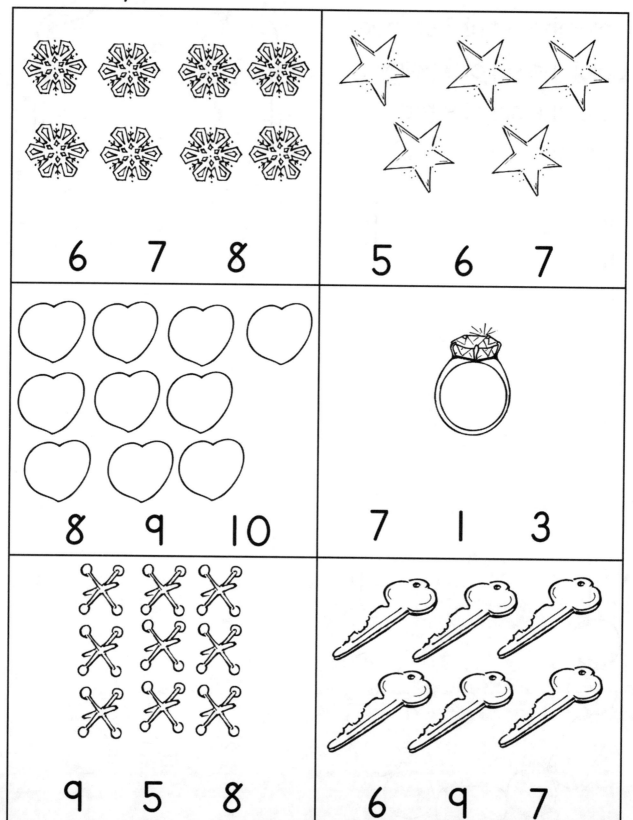

6    7    8

5    6    7

8    9    10

7    1    3

9    5    8

6    9    7

Counting objects and matching with a numeral

# Cut out the fish.
## Paste them in the correct bowls.

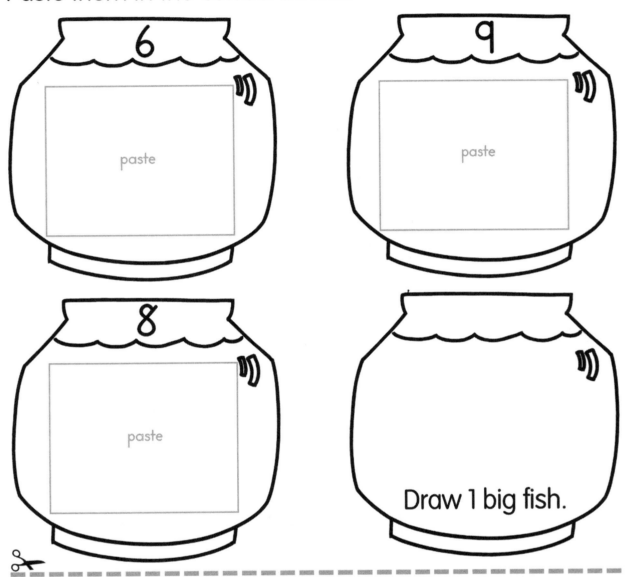

6

paste

9

paste

8

paste

Draw 1 big fish.

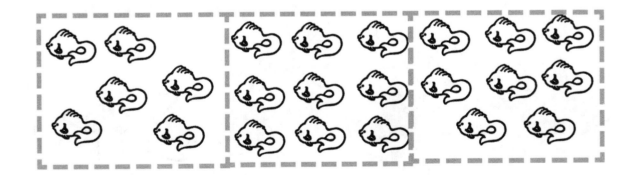

# Connect the dots.

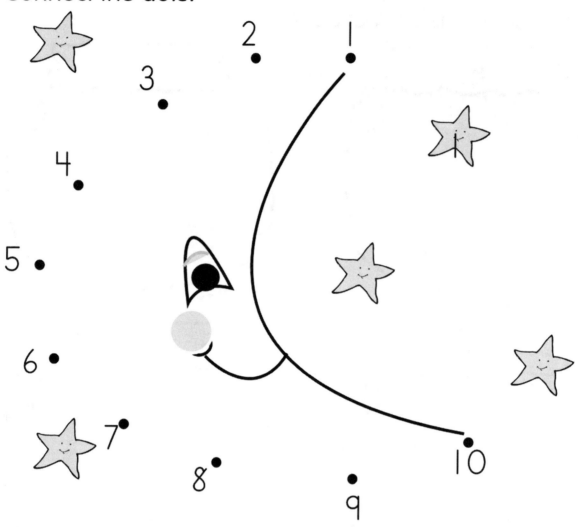

2  1

3

4

5

6

7

8

9

10

## Color me yellow.

# Cut out the numbers.
# Paste them in order.

# Fill in the missing numbers.

| 1 | 2 | 3 | 4 | 5 | 6 | 7 | 8 | 9 |

3 _____

7 _____

5 _____

8 _____

Understanding number order

# Trace and write.

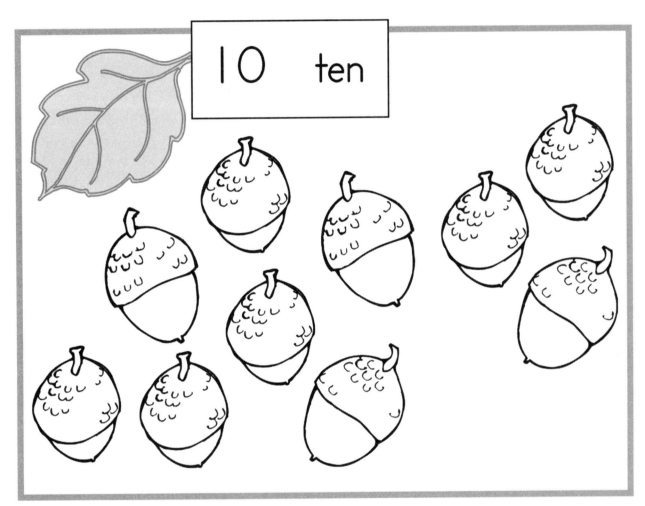

10    ten

10 10

Fill in the missing numbers.

1 ____ ____ 4 ____

____ 7 ____ 9 ____

# Connect the dots.

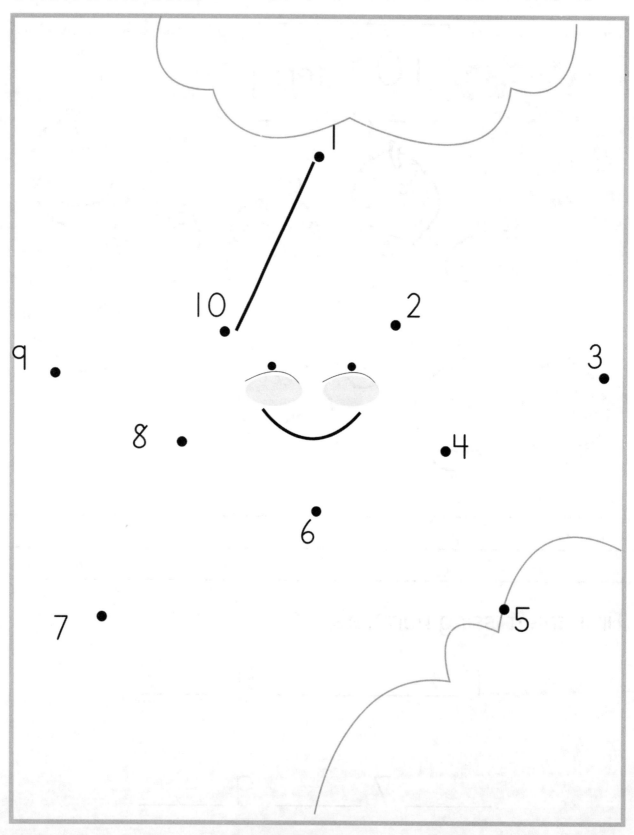

Understanding number order

# Cut out the numbers.
# Paste them in order.

# Fill in the missing numbers.

1 2 3 4 5 6 7 8 9 10

4 ___ 6

8 ___ 10

1 ___ 3

6 ___ 8

3 ___ 5

7 ___ 9

Understanding number order

# Draw the correct number of seeds.

10

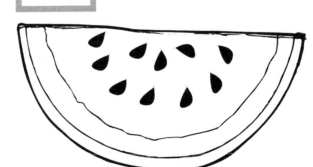

6

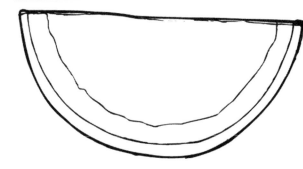

8

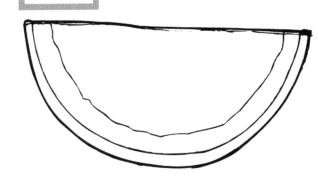

9

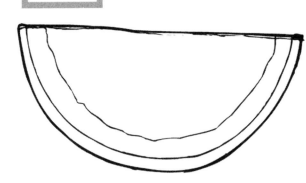

5

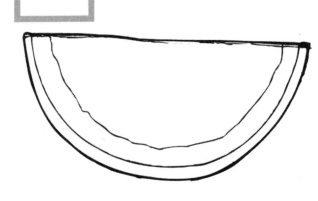

7

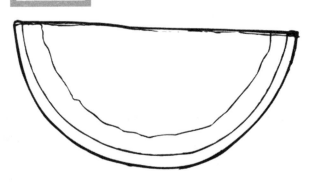

Drawing objects to match a given number

# Connect the dots and color.

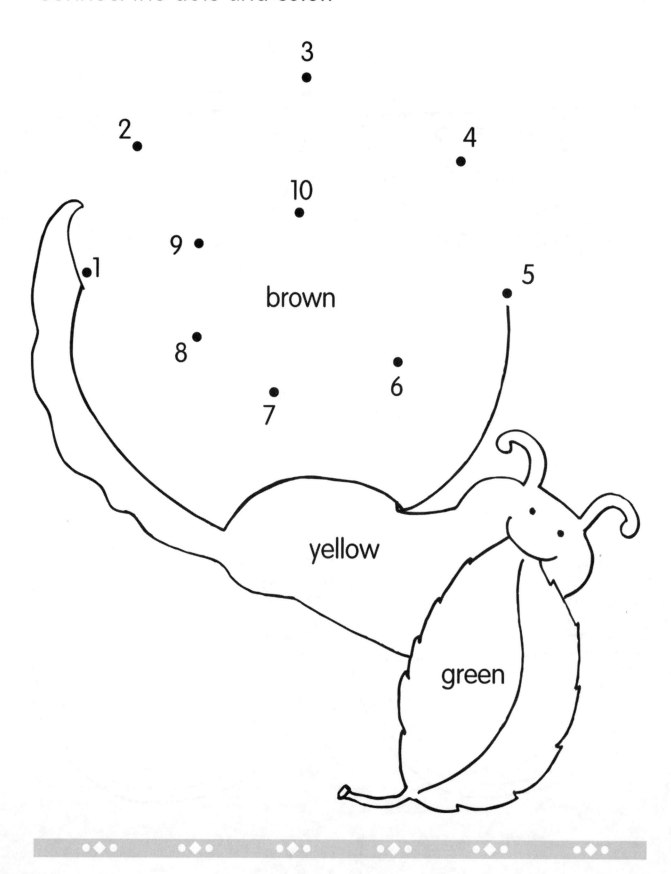

Understanding number order

# Color the picture.

2 - brown
4 - red
6 - green
8 - blue
10 - yellow

# How many are in each set?

8    9    10

5    6    7

6    7    8

10    8    9

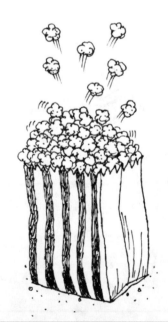

8    10    9

Counting objects and matching with a numeral

# Circle the set in each row that has **more** objects.

Getting Ready for Math

# Circle the set in each row that has the **most** objects.

Identifying the set with the most objects

# Circle the set in each row that has **fewer** objects.

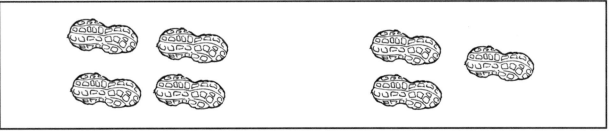

Identifying the set with fewer objects

# Circle the set in each row that has the **fewest** objects.

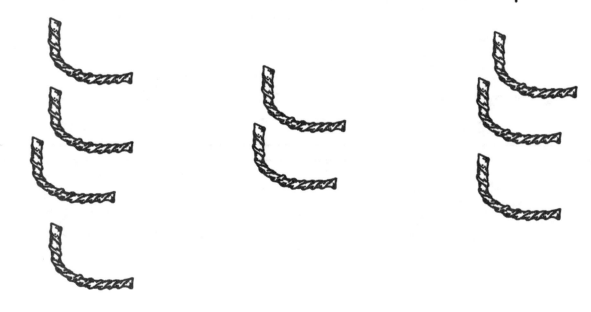

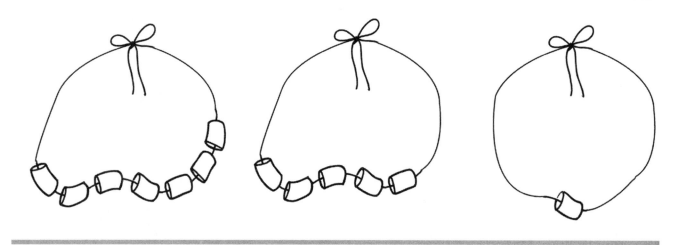

Identifying the set with the fewest objects

Color the first balloon red.

Color the second balloon blue.

Color the third balloon yellow.

Color the fourth balloon brown.

Color the fifth balloon orange.

Color. 

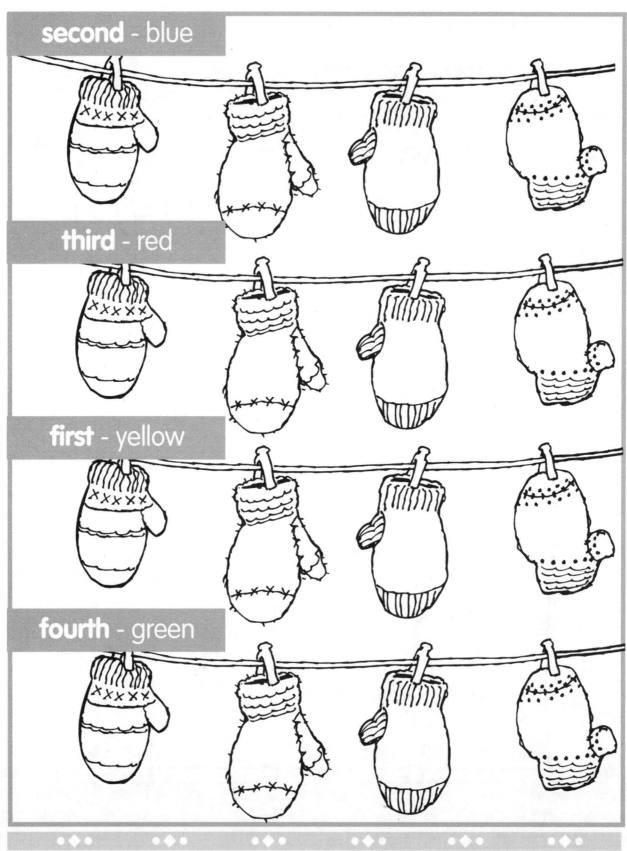

**second** - blue

**third** - red

**first** - yellow

**fourth** - green

Understanding ordinal numbers first through fourth

# Count the money.

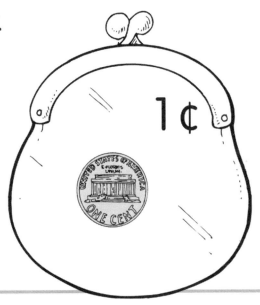

   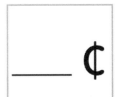

Counting pennies; recognizing the symbol for cent

# Match.

1 ¢

5 ¢

3 ¢

7 ¢

4 ¢

10 ¢

Counting penny sets and matching them with numerals

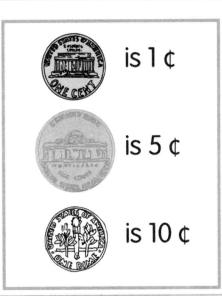

is 1 ¢

is 5 ¢

is 10 ¢

Circle 1 ¢

Circle 5 ¢

Circle 2 ¢

Circle 3 ¢

Circle 5 ¢

Circle 10 ¢

Understanding the worth of pennies, nickels, and dimes

Color the circles.

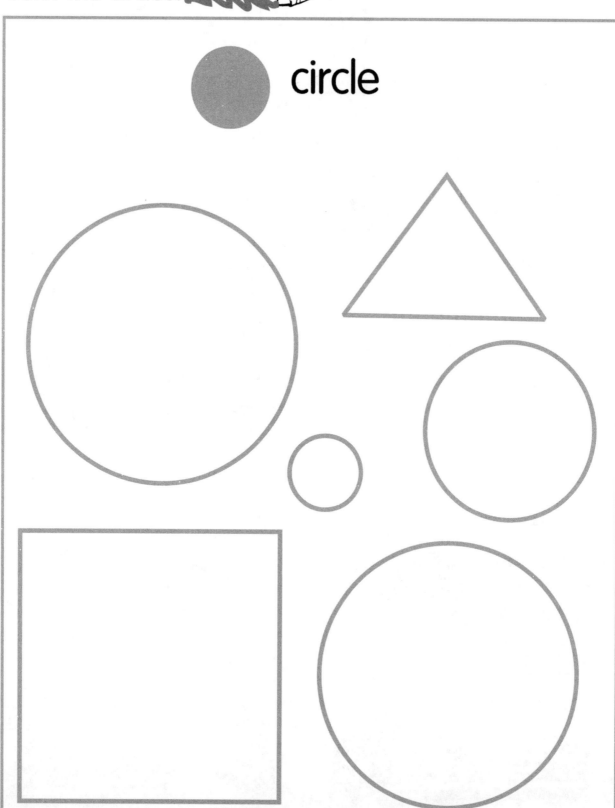

circle

Distinguishing circles from other shapes

# Color the squares.

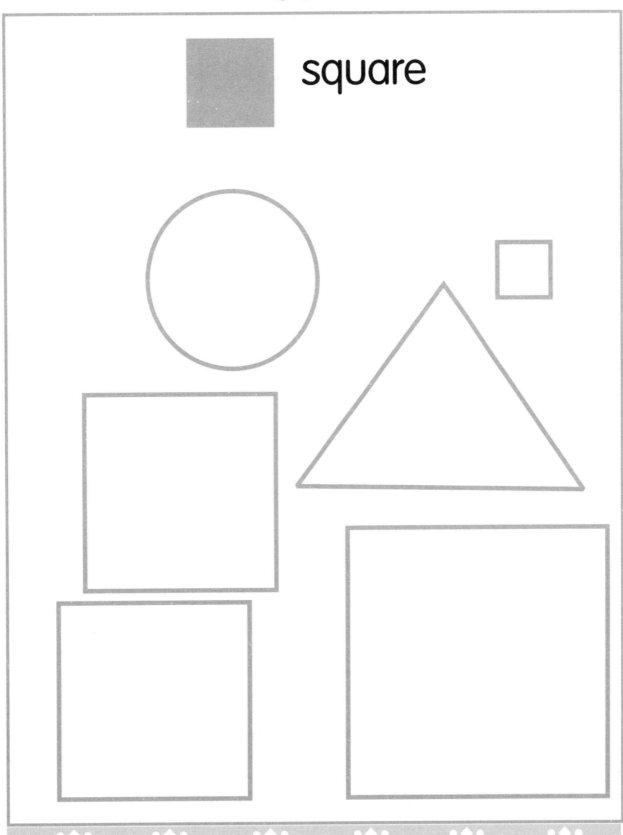

square

Getting Ready for Math

Color the triangles.

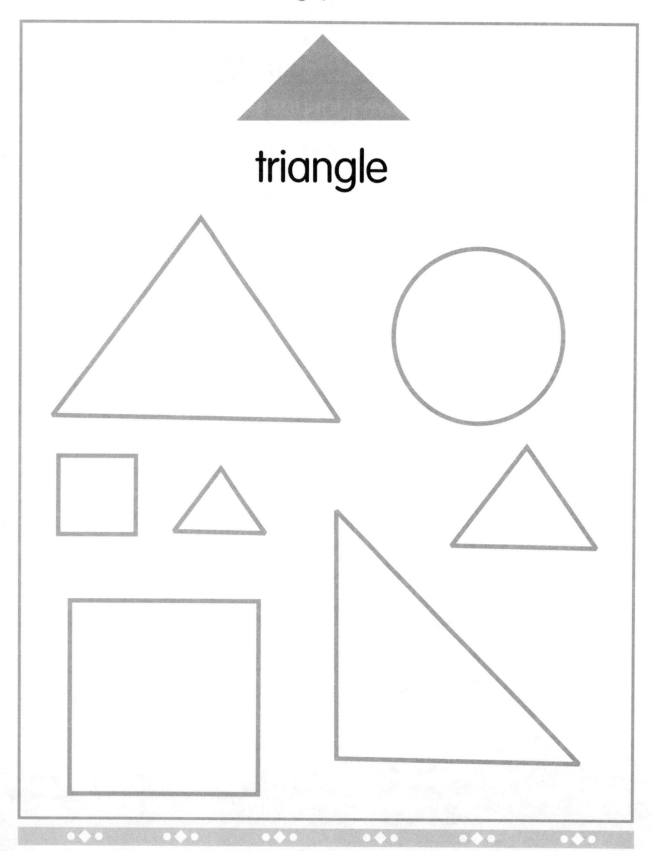

triangle

Distinguishing triangles from other shapes

# Match.

Matching shapes

# Trace and draw.

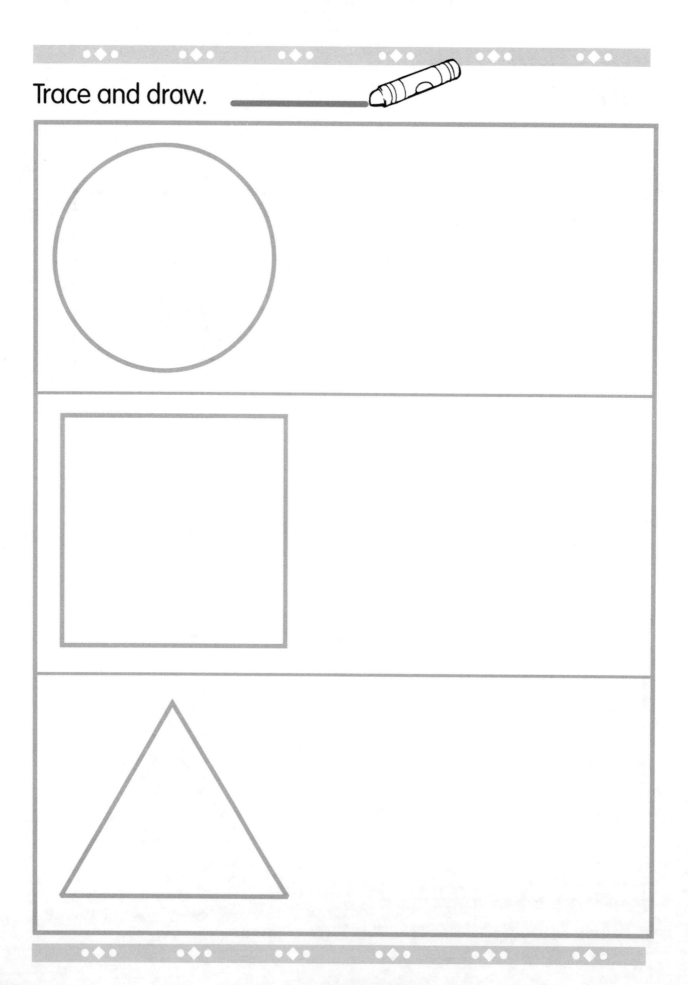

Tracing and drawing shapes

Color.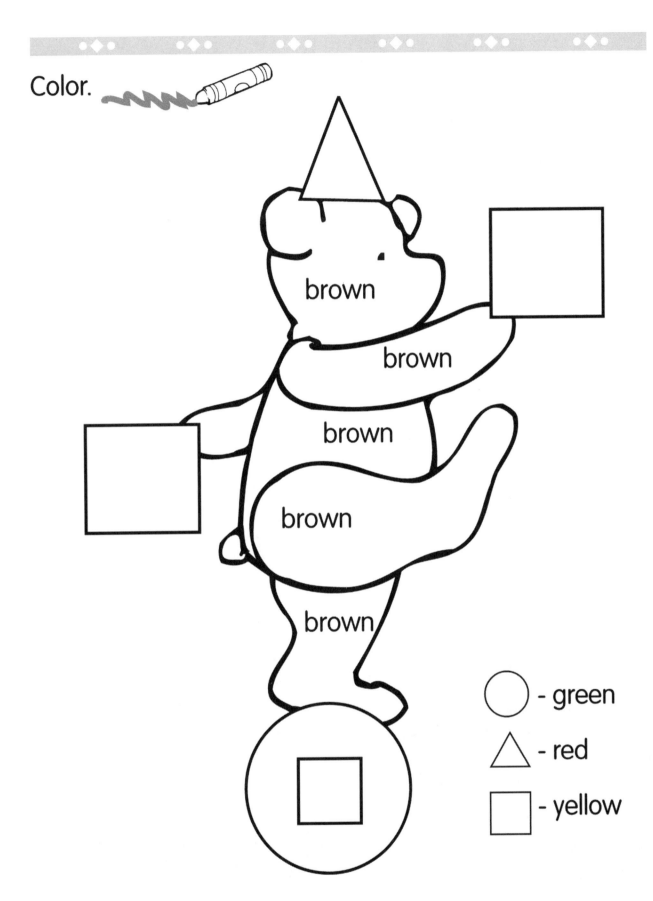

brown

brown

brown

brown

brown

◯ - green

△ - red

▢ - yellow

Recognizing shapes; following directions

# This clock tells time.
## Trace the numbers.

Tracing numbers on a clock face

# Color the biggest thing in each row.

Getting Ready for Math

# Draw an X on the smallest thing in each row.

Identifying the smallest object in a group

# Color the tallest thing in each row.

# Draw an X on the shortest thing in each row.

Identifying the shortest object in a group

# Using Number Cards

Cut the number cards apart. Use them for practice in identifying numbers and what they represent.

### Read the Numbers
Show the cards one at a time. Ask your child to give its name.

### How Much Is It?
Give your child a supply of small objects (beans, pennies, elbow macaroni, etc.) and several of the number cards. The task is to read the number and place the correct number of counters on the card. Continue until all cards are completed.

### Number Sequence
Ask your child to place the cards in numerical order from one to ten.

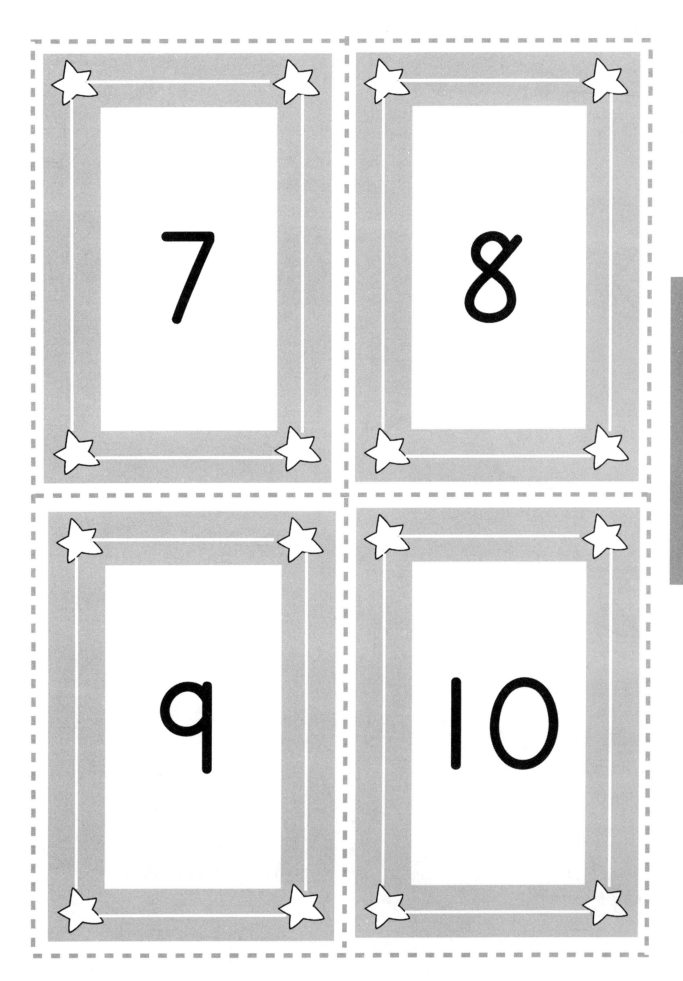

# Answer Key

Please take time to go over the work your child has completed. Ask your child to explain what he/she has done. Praise both success and effort. If mistakes have been made, explain what the answer should have been and how to find it. Let your child know that mistakes are a part of learning. The time you spend with your child helps let him/her know you feel learning is important.

**page 258**

**page 260**

**page 261**

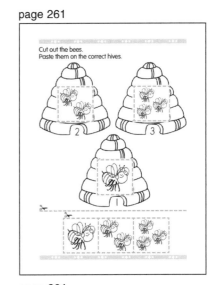

**page 262**

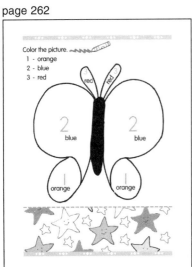

**page 263**

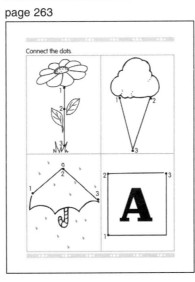

**page 264**

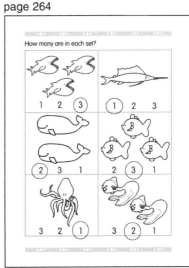

**page 266**

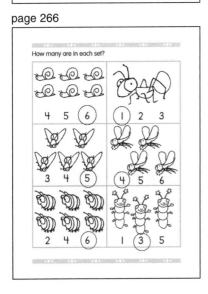

**page 267**

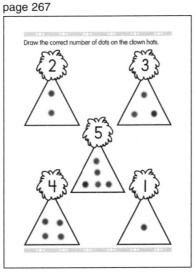

**page 268**

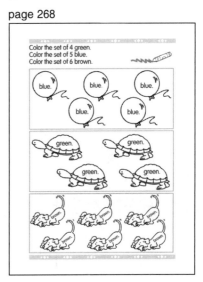

page 269

Cut out the apples.
Paste them on the correct trees.

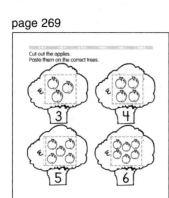

page 270

Connect the dots.

dog

page 271

Color the picture.
1 - green
2 - yellow
3 - orange

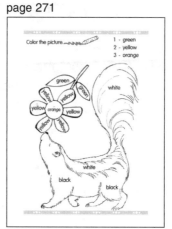

page 272

How many are in each set?

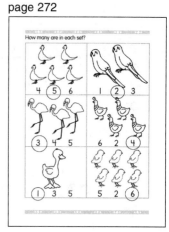

page 273

Cut out the numbers.
Paste them in order.

page 274

Fill in the missing numbers.

1 2 3 4 5 6

page 275

Draw the correct number of petals on the flowers.

page 277

Color the set of 6 purple.
Color the set of 7 orange.
Color the set of 8 yellow.
Color the set of 9 red.

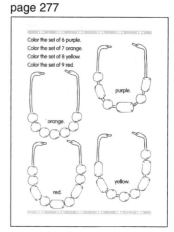

page 278

How many are in each set?

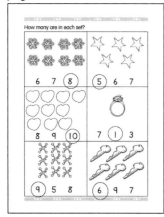

page 279

Cut out the fish.
Paste them in the correct bowls.

page 280

Connect the dots.

yellow.

Color me yellow.

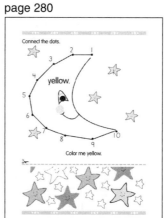

page 281

Cut out the numbers.
Paste them in order.

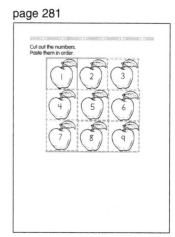

page 282

Fill in the missing numbers.

1 2 3 4 5 6 7 8 9

page 283

Trace and write.

10 ten

Fill in the missing numbers.

1 2 3 4 5
6 7 8 9 10

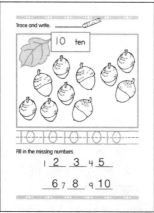

page 284

Connect the dots.

page 285

Cut out the numbers.
Paste them in order.

318                                              Answers

**page 286**

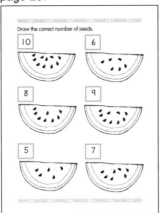

**page 287**

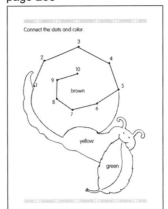

**page 288**

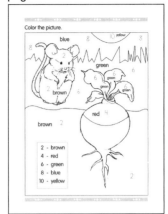

**page 289**

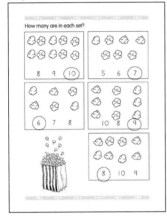

**page 290**

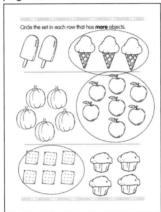

**page 291**

**page 292**

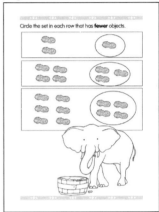

**page 293**

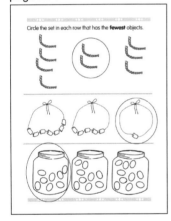

**page 294**

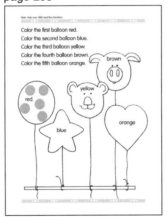

**page 295**

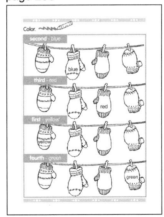

**page 296**

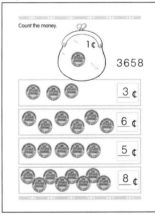

**page 297**

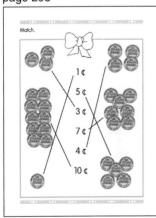

**page 298**

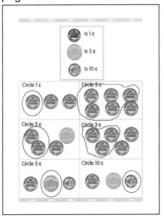

**page 299**

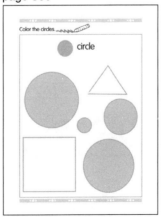

**page 300**

**page 301**

Getting Ready for Math

page 302

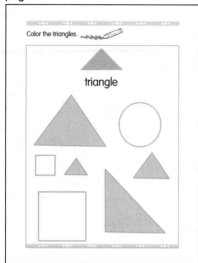

Color the triangles.

triangle

page 303

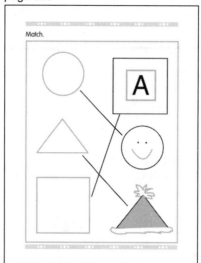

Match.

A

page 305

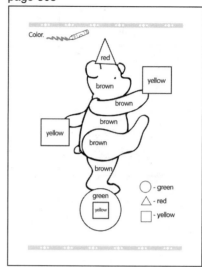

Color.

red
brown        yellow
brown
brown
yellow
brown
brown
green
yellow

○ - green
△ - red
□ - yellow

page 307

Color the biggest thing in each row.

page 308

Draw an X on the smallest thing in each row.

page 309

Color the tallest thing in each row.

page 310

Draw an X on the shortest thing in each row.

**320**                              Answers